The

Wawa®
Way

The Wawa® Way

How a Funny Name & 6 Core Values

Revolutionized Convenience

HOWARD STOECKEL *with* BOB ANDELMAN

RUNNING PRESS
PHILADELPHIA · LONDON

Books published by Running Press are available at special discounts for
bulk purchases in the United States by corporations, institutions, and other
organizations. For more information, please contact the Special Markets
Department at the Perseus Books Group, 2300 Chestnut Street, Suite 200,
Philadelphia, PA 19103, or call (800) 810-4145, ext. 5000, or e-mail
special.markets@perseusbooks.com.

ISBN 978-0-7624-5922-3
Library of Congress Control Number: 2015952690

9   8   7   6   5   4   3   2   1
Digit on the right indicates the number of this printing

Cover by Whitney Cookman
Interior design by Maria Taffera Lewis
Edited by Zachary Leibman
Typography: Futura, Universe Condensed, and Graham

Running Press Book Publishers
2300 Chestnut Street
Philadelphia, PA 19103-4371

Visit us on the web!
www.runningpress.com

For Grahame and Dick Wood,

True servant leaders,

And for every generation of Wawa associates,

Past, present, and future.

Contents

Foreword

Philadelphia Inquirer columnist Anthony Wood once described me as a "Wawa recidivist."

Guilty as charged!

While the term recidivist is normally associated with the act of repeating undesirable behavior, I choose to use the medical definition of a recidivist: "One who relapses into a previous behavior or condition." In addition to leading several educational programs for Wawa associates, I visit a Wawa store at least once a day and am one of the company's more than 1.1 million Facebook fans.

This book is about the unique Wawa retail culture. Normally, I define *culture* as what happens when the boss is not around. However, Wawa's servant leadership ensures that there are no "bosses" in the traditional sense. Rather, everyone in this great organization serves one another and the customer in a caring and consistent manner.

My definition of a *leader* is a preacher of vision, a lover of change, and a servant to others. Servant leadership is a state of mind, not a position. While Howard Stoeckel, the author of *The Wawa Way,* and Grahame Wood and Dick Wood before him led the company to its first fifty years of success (before handing the baton to Chris Gheysens), every one of the 21,000 Wawa associates defines and lives the Wawa culture of serving others.

In Thomas Kuhn's landmark book, *The Structure of Scientific Revolutions,* he posits that every significant breakthrough throughout history is in reality a "break with" old ways of thinking and old ways of doing things. With new thinking, new ways of doing, new ways of engaging associates, and prudent risk taking, the "Wawa way" has revolutionized the convenience store business. In many respects, this book you are reading is the modern-day equivalent of Sam Walton's classic autobiography, *Sam Walton, Made in America: My Story.* In his book, Walton shared the recipe for success that transformed retailing forever. He left us with ten essential rules for building a business. In *The Wawa Way,* via Wawa's six core values and their execution, Howard Stoeckel provides a blueprint for success not only for convenience stores but for every organization seeking success beyond the next quarter's sales and profits.

Howard shares many of his experiences—most successful, some not—to communicate the values of servanthood, community, colleagueship, friendship, integrity, and excellence. He does so with a spirit of humility that may be his most endearing characteristic.

I believe the real draw of this terrific book is its spirit. Be open to the feeling it creates inside you while reading it. If you do, you will become engaged and inspired. I have been blessed to have personally experienced the Wawa spirit for fifty years. However, the first time I read this book, I was reminded that serving is the true purpose of life and how an organization such as Wawa, with its culture and engaged associates, remains viable in an evolving economic, social, and global environment.

The Wawa Way is not simply an engaging story (although it is); it is a message of success that emanates from the hearts and souls of people who have lived its six core values and learned from the lessons of flying geese. It is the Wawa way or model, shared with us in a most detailed and useful way, even though Wawa's servant leaders will be the first to admit that they are far from perfect and far from complete.

Howard Stoeckel is uniquely qualified to tell this story as he draws upon his various roles in an organization with a fifty-year history of delighting customers in an ever-changing industry. While most modern organizations measure success a quarter at a time, Wawa measures success a quarter century at a time. We can all learn a great deal from Howard's humble servant leadership and Wawa's legacy. As for me, I am going to enjoy a Wawa coffee and Shorti® hoagie, as I embark on my next reading of *The Wawa Way*.

Won't you join me?

Richard J. George, PhD, Wawa recidivist and fan
Professor of Food Marketing, Haub School of Business
Saint Joseph's University, Philadelphia, Pennsylvania
April 2014

Keeping her head and Wawa coffee above water, Adelina Dairman crosses Mill Street in Vincentown, New Jersey during the 2011 flood.

Photo Credit: Michael Schwartz for the *Courier-Post*

Share of Heart

Jeremy Plauche is a burly, rowdy-looking guy—six feet, maybe 300 pounds, with the bold facial hair of a modern 24-year-old—but he admits that when he was getting the Wawa logo tattooed on his right inner biceps, the second "wa" kind of hurt. It's just a little more tender in there closer to the torso. Totally worth it, though.

Plauche works night shifts for the rescue squad in Millville, New Jersey, where he also went to high school. It's a little town about 45 miles south of Philadelphia, with a population of roughly 27,000 and four Wawas within about two miles. He's made countless Wawa runs. He's candid about his favorite product: "I'll be honest with you—the peach iced tea."

"I'm originally from Louisiana," he says. "I tried to explain to my friends there what Wawa was and what it means to people who live up here . . . and they kind of didn't believe me. Wawa is part of our culture. It's part of our way of life."

—**Don Steinberg, "It's a Wawa World,"** *Philadelphia Magazine,* **August 2011**

T*he Wawa Way* is not simply a motto, a slogan, or the title of a business book—it's a way of life, a guide for valuing people, and a road map for building long-standing customer and community relationships. So it's no coincidence that on the occasion of Wawa's fiftieth anniversary, this book has become a reality.

Today, many retail businesses measure excellence by share of market: the percentage of total sales in a specific category that they control at any one time. Banks tend to measure success by share of wallet, and public companies by their share price. At Wawa, our measure of success has always come from a more human place—one that values people, not simply profit. We strive for something we believe is more important and more enduring: share of heart.

Companies that endear themselves to customers strive for a share of their heart. To earn it, organizations such as ours must make a personal and emotional connection. We need to satisfy a need. We need to be part of the community in which our customers live. And it needs to be much more than a buy-sell relationship; it should be a partnership, friends and neighbors serving friends and neighbors. Customers will then reward us with a larger share of what's in their wallets.

(And when retailers do something wrong, customers are much more understanding of companies that have won a share of heart from them.)

If we were to pursue a share of heart relationship without building a strong foundation beneath it, ultimately the company would not endure.

The depth of passion and loyalty of Wawa customers has never ceased to amaze me. I know of no other company that receives such creative and surprising displays of affection and love from their customers. There are plenty of examples:

- The US military contingent stationed in Iraq that listed Wawa coffee at the top of their list of things they missed most.

- The long line of customers who camped out overnight to be first in line at the Wawa grand opening in Florida.
- The rock band that wrote a tribute song performed at a Wawa Hoagiefest event.
- The many couples who have chosen to have wedding photos taken at the Wawa store where they met—or even to hold the entire ceremony there.
- The five Wawa customers who together completed an almost two-year trek to visit every Wawa in existence—then 586 stores—to honor their friend's memory and raise awareness for cancer research.
- The high school graduates who regularly choose a college based at least partly on campus proximity to a Wawa.
- The University of Maryland students who, when the company announced it would close an on-campus Wawa in 2007, flash mobbed the closing store to share their memories.
- The Wawa Facebook fans (one million and counting) who share their Wawa experiences around the clock, along with the splinter groups like People Who Miss Wawa (after moving away from our six-state realm) and If Wawa Was a Person I Would Get Married to It.
- The woman who, with the help of startled Wawa associates and customers, delivered her baby in a Wawa parking lot as she made one last stop on her way to the hospital.
- The group of friends whose love for Wawa beverages resulted in their saving their 64-ounce Wawa iced-tea beverage containers and building a couch solely out of the bottles. They called it the Wawa 64 couch, only permitting a select few to sit on it.

Part of what makes us special is our name. When people hear *Wawa* for the first time, many don't know what to think. They are not sure whether it's a play on words or an improper pronunciation of a thirst quencher, but there's no doubt that many find it funny.

The origin of the name is actually fairly straightforward. Over a hundred years ago, our original dairy farm was built on land located in a rural section of Pennsylvania called Wawa, named by a local resident after the Canadian geese who flocked to a mill pond near Chester Creek.

Today, the name Wawa has come to symbolize the very best attributes of our company. Like a majestic flock of Canada geese flying synchronously in V formation, we employ the principles of teamwork, consensus, and mutual encouragement to keep our company flying high and moving swiftly. We think it's the only way to fly.

When Grahame Wood opened the first Wawa store, he thought that it might be wise to have a more generic-sounding name that evoked the quick in-and-out convenience of our stores. But Grahame ended up sticking with Wawa because it was memorable and distinguished our stores from others. It's a suitable name for our company because it's intentionally noncorporate and actually fun to say.

I get such a thrill out of telling people I work for Wawa. They most always respond in the same way: "Wawa? I *love* Wawa!" That kind of fierce loyalty and intense emotion lets me know that they are not just buying their coffee or food there. It tells me that we've connected with them at a deeper level, well beyond their mind or their wallet, to a rare and special place: their heart.

Share of heart means customers referring to their Wawa as "my Wawa." Shopping at Wawa is part of our customers' daily routine. It's a habit-forming experience. It's like getting up and turning on the news, or logging on to Facebook for a daily fix of friends and family status updates. It becomes part of our customers' lives.

When you share part of a customer's heart, the service relationship changes. Customers become friends—and in many cases more like family members.

In Aston, Pennsylvania, one of our customers had cancer and was unable to physically get to the store. When Wawa associates from our Aston store 8027 heard about it, they adopted him and made certain that every day he received what he wanted in the store, in some cases delivering products to his home. Once recovered, he gave the store tremendous credit for lifting his spirits and helping him get back on his own two feet. It was the encouragement and the therapy he needed during a very difficult time.

This is one of the thousands of stories that play out across the company every day, year after year. In *The Wawa Way*, we'll share more stories like this one and show how this kind of connection can make a company truly special—and very successful.

· · · · ·

I imagine that people who know me sometimes wonder how in the world a C student and former bellhop from New Jersey got lucky enough to run one of the best companies in the world. I'd say it came down to a little luck, good timing, and a whole lot of heart.

I served as a Wawa company executive for twenty-five years, including being CEO from 2005 to 2012. This is not a position I ever imagined myself in. I lack the elite background of many corporate CEOs. I was not the captain of any football team or a member of any honor society. In fact, I barely made it through high school. My teachers told me to take wood shop, commenting, "You would be better using hammers and saws than textbooks." When there was no red ink on my report card, believe me, there was relief in the Stoeckel household. I don't recall what my class rank was in high school, but it was perpetually near the bottom. It was a cliffhanger as to whether or not I'd graduate, but in the end I squeaked through.

What turned me around was a job as a bellhop at a Howard Johnson motel. That's how I got turned on to business. I was inspired enough to defy the odds and enroll in Rider College in Lawrenceville, New Jersey. I got off to a slow start but eventually worked my way up to assistant manager of the motel. Something about serving others appealed to me. Somehow I found my way and the sense of a higher calling, which I'd been lacking in high school.

I earned a bachelor of science degree in commerce from Rider with a major in business administration. I went on to work as an executive trainee at the John Wanamaker department store in Philadelphia, where I learned about the benefits of a family-run business. Then I moved on to The Limited in Columbus, Ohio, and Boston, where I learned about publicly traded business.

I finally landed at Wawa in the human resources department. Ultimately, I moved from vice president of human resources to vice president of marketing to CEO. At each step, I found I could be myself, serve others, and make a difference. In Wawa, I'd found a company that truly valued people—a company that believed ordinary people could achieve the extraordinary. Even better, I'd found my passion; it's a feeling that resonates beneath everything that happens at Wawa.

In this book you'll read about a lot of ordinary people who've achieved extraordinary things. Many of the stories that follow were shared over a cup of coffee in the local Wawa, or they are letters from customers received at our call center, or postings on our website, but they are all part of Wawa's shared history. And you'll read about what has led to Wawa's success during the past half century—no doubt the same things that will drive results in the future. It's not rocket science. It's not algorithms. It really comes down to something that's much more common, something that empowers the ordinary to become extraordinary. We call it the Wawa way.

In a two-year study of world-class service in convenience retail, researchers with the *Harvard Business Review* ranked Wawa's customer service in a league with Nordstrom and the Ritz-Carlton: "They consider employees their living brand and devote a great deal of time and energy to training and developing them so that they reflect the brand's core values. In fact, these companies make as much effort to groom employees as they do to develop pithy messages about what the brand is and does."

The Wawa way is our living and breathing recipe for success. It is built upon three fundamental elements that seem to fly in the face of traditional corporate success:

- a business model of private and shared ownership
- a management philosophy of servant leadership
- a culture driven by six core values

Private ownership lets us take a long-term point of view that is not tied to the whims of Wall Street. Shared ownership allows us to deepen the commitment of our team members and share the risks and rewards across our entire company. Our core values have been the company's touchstone since its founding.

In the pages that follow, we'll share the details of this recipe with you. *The Wawa Way* is more than a history book. It's a handbook for a new era in consumer relationships where the culture and values of a company become the new measure of true and sustainable success. It's proof that a small business with a funny name and a rich history can succeed against bigger, better-funded competition—and in the process help make the world a better place.

Some call it business sense. Others call it common sense. I call it goose sense. Whatever you call it, it's the shaping force that makes the Wawa way a living, joyful reality for countless people.

Welcome to the Wawa way!

Howard Stoeckel
Wawa, Pennsylvania
April 2014

Wawa is a Native American word for
Canada goose. To us, it means convenience
and exceptional service.

CHAPTER 1

"What Is a Wawa?"

The I Love Wawa group on MySpace.com has more than 5,000 members, making it the largest of several Wawa-related groups on the online-community site. Over on Livejournal.com, there's a group called We Love Wawa, with about 950 members. This would be pretty ho-hum if Wawa were an indie band or video game. Instead, it's a chain of convenience stores.

—Rob Walker, "Convenience Cult?" *New York Times,* July 30, 2006

The name always catches people off guard. "What the heck is a Wawa?" they ask.

And it's not just our funny name. One of the downsides of having such a unique and special store is that it's often hard to describe to people who don't already know us. We're not a coffee shop, but we sell more coffee than many national brands. We're not a restaurant—we have no place to sit and no waitstaff—but we sell more meals than the majority of fast-food restaurants. We're not a gas station, but we sell three to four times more gas than many traditional big-name stations. And we're not exactly a convenience store, but our stores are open 24/7, 365 days a year, offering customers more ways to simplify an increasingly hectic life.

Although our core purpose is to simplify our customers' lives, our business is anything but simple. We serve more than 500 million customers a year, and we are known for our Wawa-branded products, like teas, milk, coffee, and freshly made hoagies and sandwiches. (Hoagie is a regional name for the classic Italian sandwich also known as a sub, grinder, or hero.) Traditionally, hoagies are built-to-order sandwiches filled with fresh meats and cheeses as well as lettuce, tomatoes, and onions, topped off with a dash of oregano on an Italian roll. As you'll learn in this book, hoagies have become a big, much-beloved part of Wawa's brand identity. Those daily purchases add up to 190 million cups of coffee and 60 million sandwiches a year. At our surcharge-free ATMs, there are more than 75 million transactions a year. We also sell 1.8 percent of all the automotive fuel purchased in the United States.

When we started in the convenience store business in 1964, we were the alternative to a supermarket that was then operating on limited hours and not open on Sundays. People would stop on their way home, grab deli, produce, or a dairy item, and go home to enjoy it with friends or family. Over a period of time, however, we evolved into a restaurant-to-go for breakfast, lunch, and dinner, the in-between snack occasion, or an afternoon pick-me-up.

Today, our biggest competitors aren't supermarkets or even 7-Eleven; they're McDonald's, Dunkin' Donuts, and ExxonMobil.

Along the way, we went from small stores that had fifteen parking places surrounding 2,400 square-foot shops to big stores of more than 5,600 square feet with more than fifty parking places. That was a revolutionary development in the convenience store industry. We spend more on choosing locations and building stores than anyone else in our industry. Where others would spend a million or two on a single location, we spend two to three times that.

Because we're so unique, we intentionally resist labeling ourselves. Many people simply give up on describing us to their friends and just say, "You just have to go there. You'll see." Actually, they are almost correct. When a customer visits a Wawa, it's what they see, feel, taste, smell, and hear that defines our offering. It's not any single sandwich or beverage or gas price. We have always focused on the total experience.

Wawa dominates the landscape because we're a habit-forming, ritualistic type of brand. Remember the TV sitcom *Cheers*, set in the fictional Boston bar and restaurant where "everyone knows your name"? That's how many customers think of us. We're the Cheers of convenience stores, a place where you're known by name, and where the customers and associates all treat each other like family.

We're that neighborhood store; a place where Mary behind the food service counter, Pete at the specialty coffee bar, and Mimi at the cash register are all friends and neighbors, where they are known for serving their friends and neighbors each and every day.

Our customers also don't fit neatly into a single demographic box. At any one time you'll see a construction worker, a businesswoman, teens, kids, soccer moms, college students, and seniors all moving around the store like they own the place, chatting with associates, holding the doors for each other. The stores have a great community vibe that begins at dawn and lasts all through the late-night hours.

Stephen Hoch, a marketing professor at the Wharton business school, says that when you think about it, Wawa might not even be a convenience store in the traditional sense anymore—the place you'd go as a last resort for a can of soup. That role has been assumed by drugstores like CVS, Walgreen's, or the dollar stores. Really, Hoch says, "Wawa has become a fast-food restaurant with a gas station."

The equation isn't as simple as it might sound. Having gas pumps is heavy baggage for any food retailer; no gas retailer has been known for appetizing food. Made-to-order food is a complicated and ever-changing mountain to climb. Having both puts us in a space all our own with one of the highest degrees of difficulty of any retailer. We have had food inspectors in Florida who said, "I can't inspect this store because I'm a convenience store inspector. We need a restaurant inspector to come in here."

Customers share this impression. Many comment, "This is no convenience store. This is a restaurant." We like hearing that, because it tells us we're achieving a level of attractiveness, comfort, and quality that our competitors can't match. When you're in the experience business, you can never afford to become a commodity, interchangeable with any other store around the corner.

Some would say that the notion of trying to orchestrate millions of positive experiences in the face of so many variables, products, people, prices, and programs is not possible. Imagine how fast-food restaurants would fail if they also tried to sell gas outside. Imagine what people would think about buying fresh-tasting produce at a traditional gas station. Now imagine hundreds of stores doing exactly that for thousands of customers 24/7 in a way that makes everyone happy!

That's what Wawa is. More than a store, more than a favorite restaurant, more than a fast and friendly fueling stop. It's a positive part of our customers' lives. Believe me, it's not easy, but our associates creating tens of thousands of good feelings every day is our true sustainable advantage. Is there any better way to serve our communities?

In 1842, George Wood was born, and in 1902, he opened the Wawa Dairy Farms.

CHAPTER 2

Birth of a Family Business

And in flocks the wild-goose, Wawa,
Flying to the fen-lands northward.

—**Henry Wadsworth Longfellow, "The Song of Hiawatha"**

As you can imagine, a business that is unique—and uniquely successful—generally has a unique story behind it. And that's certainly the case with Wawa. It would take far more than one book to spell out everything that has happened since the Richard Wood family first moved to Philadelphia in 1682, the moment that set in motion a family business that has evolved and changed dramatically during the more than 330 years since. From the days of Lincoln to now, the Wood family's influence has been felt far beyond the borders of the Keystone State.[1]

---

1 Abraham Lincoln, incidentally, did legal work for the Wood family business before becoming the sixteenth president of the United States. The Wood family's collection of historical materials includes three letters written by Lincoln.

Today, you can find evidence of this in cities such as New Orleans and Charlottesville. There you'll see the same name stamped on many of these cities' original fire hydrants: RD Wood & Co.[2] The Wood family is no longer in the business of making fire hydrants, but this history is still very important to Wawa today. For a company that remains privately held, this rich heritage holds lessons about adaptation and the importance of change that its leaders still use as a point of reference.

After arriving in Philadelphia, succeeding generations of the Wood family crossed the Delaware River into southern New Jersey, settling by 1716 in what is now Cumberland County. They farmed and got into a variety of occupations that centered on shipping produce and cedar logs to communities all along the Delaware Bay. Eventually, another Richard Wood established a store (it still stands today) in Greenwich on the Cohansey River. Two of his sons, David and Richard, who would play roles in the businesses that spawned Wawa, got their starts in that little store on the corner of Ye Great Street and Bacon's Neck Road.

David C. Wood branched out, opening his own stores in nearby communities and expanding his trade to include such exotic imports as Spanish "segars," watches, and a full line of household china. In 1803, he and a partner saw opportunity in the growing demand for decorative and utilitarian cast-iron products that could be made using local bog iron. They constructed a foundry and furnace on the Maurice River in Millville and opened an office on Water Street in Philadelphia to market their wares. The furnace and foundry produced stove plates, fire backs, fence posts, and water pipe, which was timely because many cities were busy replacing old wooden water pipe systems. Millville Furnace ultimately shipped pipe to many cities along the Atlantic coast.

David's younger brother, Richard, known as R.D., was a brilliant

---

2 These and many other historic details about Wawa's past come from *Wawa: Images of America*, by Maria M. Thompson and Donald H. Price, Arcadia Publishing, 2004.

businessman with a knack for seeing possibilities and a willingness to take calculated risks. While still quite young, he left his father's Greenwich store for Salem, a prosperous market town in Salem County, and soon afterward moved to Philadelphia where, with partners, he opened a dry goods store on Market Street. At the time, dry goods merchants might carry an array of products as varied as lead and paint pigments, toweling, and cotton sheeting. Wood even became involved in importing English woolen blankets that he had made in various weights and shipped to communities from New Orleans to Canada. He traveled extensively to secure customers and service accounts. His natural curiosity, personal discipline, and widespread knowledge of the country combined with his business interests led him to get involved in activities ranging from a canal company to a glassworks.

R.D. Wood bought Millville Furnace with its vast landholdings in 1850 from David and immediately modernized the ironworks. The grist and sawmills got a makeover, too, and Wood realized that the waterpower generated by the Maurice River could support more milling activity. Following the maxim "grow what you know," he decided to manufacture cotton textiles and built a complex that included a mill and, later, a bleachery and dye works. He named the factories New Jersey Mills at Millville, but as the businesses grew, the iron and textile branches of the enterprise gained individual identities: RD Wood & Co. manufactured iron pipe and other iron products and the Millville Manufacturing Company produced cotton textiles. Wood had six sons and he oversaw their participation in his businesses.

By the late 1880s, R.D.'s son George was head of a large and thriving business as well as a growing family that spent summers at various locations outside Philadelphia. In 1889, the family stayed at the Idlewild Hotel in Media, and George often rode on horseback through the surrounding countryside. He must have liked what he saw, because the following summer he rented a rambling Victorian house with a colorful red roof in a Delaware County community known by the name of its rail station: Wawa. He subsequently bought the house and called it Red Roof. Today, it and other buildings on the site are home to Wawa's corporate headquarters.

At Wawa, George Wood indulged his interest in farming and raising dairy cows. He purchased land near his summer house and by the turn of the century was ready to become a serious gentleman farmer. In 1900, he bought three adjoining parcels of land in neighboring Middletown Township, including Rocky Run Dairy Farm. George formulated a business plan, hired an architect, built a sanitary dairy, began importing purebred Guernsey cows, and established a distribution system. By 1902, Wawa Dairy Farms was up and running.

Prior to the introduction of pasteurization, the dairy operation specialized in "certified" raw milk products like milk, cream, cottage cheese, and buttermilk that were iced down throughout the bottling and distribution process. Wawa advertised its "super safe" perishable products through professional medical societies and physicians' offices. That might sound strange to modern ears, but in the early days of the twentieth century, milk wasn't a popular table drink. It was consumed mostly by babies, small children, and invalids, so a guarantee of healthy cows, sanitary milking and bottling conditions, and proper storage and transport was critical to marketing efforts. Years later, FRESH FROM THE COUNTRY would be emblazoned on the side of tractor trailers delivering Wawa products to Wawa stores, and the slogan was as true then as it had been at the turn of the twentieth century.

As time went by, tastes changed. Commercial milk products such as cottage cheese and buttermilk, along with milk and cream, gained widespread popularity. Wawa was ready. The company expanded its retail routes to include developing communities just outside Philadelphia city limits.

A Little Piece of History: The Wawa Milk Truck

In the early 1990s, Wawa wanted to restore one of its original milk delivery trucks to show at store openings and community events. Wawa searched far and wide and finally found a 1918 autocar at the bottom of an abandoned coal mine in central Pennsylvania.

Wawa shipped the truck's rusty carcass to restoration experts in Lebanon, Pennsylvania. Three months later, the entire truck had been disassembled, sanded, and repainted. Each part of the truck was hung separately from the rafters in a barn in Lebanon before the entire vehicle was reassembled piece by piece, its woodwork and leather entirely replaced with new material.

The truck still works to this day and appears at Wawa celebrations to remind our new associates and customers about our dairy history and our long-standing commitment to quality.

For those traveling who couldn't live without Wawa milk products, they could be shipped by rail or aboard ocean liners.

Wawa's business has evolved dramatically in the years since then. But dairy products continue to play an important role in our operations. Each year, the Wawa Dairy produces more than 40 million gallons of beverages, and not only milk. Our teas are fantastically popular, for no other reason than they are delicious and remind people of home. College students ask parents to ship them Wawa tea. They're often one of the first products people get when they enter the market. In Florida, we opened our stores without our Wawa line of teas and customers demanded them! We responded by trucking them down to Florida to satisfy their thirst for Wawa beverages. In this way, the dairy business that George Wood founded over a century ago continues to delight our customers.

George Wood died in 1926, leaving the businesses in the care of his two sons. But before he died he established several trusts, one of which still endures. The trust ensures the continued involvement of Wood's descendants in the ownership of the company and enables management to plan and make decisions for the long term. The trust is a key feature in the structure of Wawa that helps make it an especially effective—and the much beloved—business organization.

Two years after George's death, new state regulations about the storage and processing of milk required a new dairy to be built. Wawa's iconic brick plant on US Route 1 was built in 1929 at a cost of $250,000. The state-of-the-art plant was featured on the cover of *Milk Plant Monthly* in June 1933.

However, even with all the modern innovations, things were not so rosy. The general economic depression took its toll, and it was expensive to maintain a farm and dairy in the country, then truck the milk to Philadelphia to be loaded on home delivery trucks. Profits suffered. World War II brought its own set of challenges—reduced consumption, rationing, and workers who left employment to serve their country. Contracts with big customers such as the Philadelphia Naval Shipyard temporarily helped save the day. But when the war ended, Wawa was forced to sell some of its equipment and property.

It was at this time that John J. Finley Jr. was put in charge of the dairy operation, and he began making improvements to the business. According to a speech given by Grahame Wood in 1975, Finley oversaw a series of mergers and acquisitions throughout the 1950s that included Crystle Dairy, Ardrossan, Brookmead, and Turner & Wescott. In the height of door-to-door delivery during the late 1940s and 50s, Wawa mobilized between

The Trusted Milkman

Wawa milkman Tom Summers epitomized the home delivery salesman of the 1950s. A veteran of World War II, he was drawn to the work because he liked the schedule of five weeks on and one week off, as well as the independence and responsibility of keeping track of accounts, collecting money, and turning it in. This entrepreneurial spirit was bolstered by raffles and promotions designed to attract new customers and introduce existing customers to additional dairy products. Milkmen like Tom were frequently entrusted with keys to a customer's house and, on occasion, they performed truly heroic feats. Driver Frank Verna received the Pasteur Award as an outstanding humanitarian for rescuing a family of three small children from a burning building.

seventy and eighty drivers. The drivers earned the trust of their customers and communities.

However, demand for home delivery of dairy products was dwindling. Newly prosperous Americans were moving to the suburbs and buying their milk at the vast new supermarkets. By the end of the decade, Wawa was confronted by the toughest business questions of all: What is our market? Who are our customers, and how can we serve them best?

Enter Grahame Wood, the man who changed Wawa forever.

On April 16, 1964, in Folsom, Pennsylvania,
Wawa opened the doors of its first-ever food market.

CHAPTER 3

Coining the Convenience Concept

Rich George noticed the brand-new Wawa store, not far from his house, and wondered what the milkmen were doing selling groceries. That was 45 years ago, when Wawa meant uniformed men delivering glass bottles of milk, a delta of cream on top; when the subtle clinking of glass outside front doors and vestibules might be the first clue that daylight was spreading across the sky. In 1964, the inelegant terms Wawa and grocery might have been incongruous. But George, a professor of food marketing at St. Joseph's University and Wawa recidivist, now realizes he was witnessing the birth of a phenomenon, part of a burgeoning cultural shift that would redefine towns and change how people shop and eat.

—Anthony R. Wood, "How Wawa Became a Success,"
Philadelphia Inquirer, April 16, 2009

Grahame Wood, George Wood's grandson, grew up in Philadelphia and in Wawa, Pennsylvania. He graduated from the University of Pennsylvania in 1939. After college, he joined George Wood Sons & Co. and worked from the New York office.

As with many men of his generation, his career was interrupted by World War II. He served in Europe, fighting with the army's 111th Infantry Division and the 101st Airborne Division, which took him to the Battle of the Bulge and earned him a Silver Star. Military service taught Grahame the value of teamwork, and he and his paratrooper buddies enjoyed annual reunions in the decades that followed.

Grahame moved with his family back to Wawa to help care for his ailing father and so he could better oversee George Wood Sons & Co. and the family's textile manufacturing operations in New Jersey. The growth of the Millville business had stalled, and Grahame initiated discussions about the possible sale of portions of the textile operation. He also turned his eye to the dairy. He wondered, Could that business be saved?

An associate at Breyers-Sealtest suggested the possibility of company-owned stores featuring milk and ice cream based on plans for a chain of stores called Dairy Dells that Breyers had considered but shelved. Grahame studied these plans and toured stores established by High's Dairy in Washington, DC.

Grahame also had the good fortune to have a close friend whose brother lived in Cincinnati and owned seven King Kwik Minit Market stores. Grahame visited those stores and spent a week working in one of them as part of his research, returning home with the store's blueprints.

The leader in the brand new convenience store industry was 7-Eleven. Founded in 1927 in Texas as an outgrowth of an ice company, the company adopted the 7-Eleven name (for its original hours of operation) in 1946 and began opening stores in the Philadelphia market in the late 1950s and early '60s.

Outside of these few pioneering operations, very little was known about how convenience stores really worked. So when Grahame Wood presented a business plan for three experimental convenience stores in the Wawa Dairy's market area at the September 1963 board meeting, the plan was greeted with trepidation.

But they approved it. In December 1963, the dairy board of directors passed a resolution appointing Grahame Wood as chairman of the board of directors and senior executive officer of the newly christened Wawa Food Markets, a subsidiary of the Wawa Dairy.

The first store opened on MacDade Boulevard in Folsom, Pennsylvania, in Delaware County, on Thursday, April 16, 1964. Twelve years later, Wood remarked he would never forget that day:

> *The first sale was to a lady who brought to the counter a gallon of ice cream then on sale for $0.99. I took her one-dollar bill, which now hangs in a frame on the wall of my office. In my excitement and in the awe of this moment, I rang up $99 on the register. At the time neither our first customer nor I thought it was funny. At closing I counted the money and made an entry in the ledger book for the first day's sales—$359.86.*

When planning what the stores would look like, how they would be stocked, and where they would be located, Wood stuck to the things he knew and believed in. He wanted to house stores in simple, straightforward buildings, stock them with quality Wawa dairy products and other brand name staples, as well as perishable foods like produce and delicatessen meats and cheeses, and center the business in the familiar territory of Delaware County, Pennsylvania. It worked and, while times have changed and Wawa has evolved with them—it still works. The unique value proposition offered by today's Wawa has its roots in the guiding principles set out by Grahame Wood in early 1964.

The Quaker heritage of the Wood family influenced Grahame's general approach to life. He could be shy and was not one to seek the limelight. He led by example and by his very nature exemplified what is now known as servant leadership. Perhaps his natural personal style was reinforced by his military experience, in which the power of group commitment to a single, clearly defined goal made all the difference between success and failure. He was humble and, although reserved, was accessible, which made for open channels of communication.

Grahame and his wife, Emilie, were avid gardeners. Emilie tended the vegetable and flower gardens, while Grahame found joy in the propagation of azaleas, rhododendrons, and hollies. His son Fred recalled the scientific approach his father took to this avocation, not unlike the methodical, careful way he studied the data before entering the convenience store field. Grahame Wood was a natural entrepreneur who after careful study could make a decision and recommendation with confidence. He was also willing to acknowledge when things did not work. This spirit of constant analysis, experimentation, and learning infused the company culture and guided my own work as Wawa's CEO many years later.

Grahame Wood made the Wawa stores a reality. Not only did he formulate the plan but he also went to banks to secure loans. When Grahame first asked for a $50,000 loan from Philadelphia National Bank he was turned down. Undaunted, Grahame turned to Southeast National Bank to secure financing and in the end prevailed. This made the new phase of the family business possible.

The first company office consisted of a few desks in the dairy. Later the small group of employees moved to an old farmhouse, also on dairy property, while unused barns were converted to warehouses for perishables, tobacco, and candy. As the number of stores grew, the company tried new things—some with little success. There were Wawa laundromats, rug machine rentals, and short-lived kitchens featuring fried chicken, fish and chips, and hamburgers for $0.20. The company also experimented with growing hydroponic tomatoes that eventually came to an end when the greenhouse blew down in a storm. Other ideas rooted in quality and customer convenience, such as redesigned deli and checkout areas, took hold. An emphasis on clean and friendly stores morphed into the culture of today's Wawa: "Friends and neighbors serving friends and neighbors."

Little by little, the number of stores grew, and the company expanded geographically throughout southeastern Pennsylvania, New Jersey, Delaware, Maryland, and Connecticut. Grahame's store tours grew beyond Saturday-morning excursions into major fact-finding missions.

One summer, Grahame's son Fred was his driver. He recalls:

> *I took my father to visit store sites and to meet with*
> *contractors and potential landlords with whom he negotiated*
> *for new sites. He purchased a van and took the middle seat out*
> *of the back and installed a small table that was attached to one*
> *fixed wall and that was his desk . . . He would be in the back*
> *taking notes or transcribing notes to some more formal written*
> *material, or looking at property or drawings of buildings. A lot*
> *of times the conversations at lunch would be over terms and he*
> *would write those on the back of envelopes or napkins.*

This attention to detail and meticulous record keeping empowered Grahame as he guided the growing company.

Grahame made another change to the way of doing business that Dick Wood, his cousin and successor as CEO, feels was critical to the company's success. In the early 1970s, Grahame attended a symposium in Chicago on corporate governance. Those in attendance were urged to seek board members from outside the organization with business savvy who had no conflicts of interest and would be able to dispassionately evaluate company performance. Grahame returned to Wawa, implemented this "best practice" recommendation, and helped ensure that the company would receive sound advice from its directors for years to come.

Grahame Wood earned the affection and dedication of Wawa employees and staff. His good humor and sense of fun were evident at company picnics, store openings, anniversaries, employee milestones, and other celebratory occasions.

Longtime associate Joe Gallagher recalls being thrilled by Grahame's unannounced visits:

> *He would come and visit your store and no matter what was going on, you were the most important thing there. He used to have a driver—which enabled him to work while on the road—and he would come into your store, so it was really cool. I was only twenty-one years old so I was intimidated by him, by his appearance. But he cared about me. And I'll never forget as long as I live how he'd come into the store. It could have been a surprise visit or a holiday visit, but the most important thing was, "How you doing, Joe? How's everything going? What can we do for you?" And that transcended all the way through the years with Dick and with Howard.*

Area Manager Lynne Conlan tells a great Grahame story about when she was an associate in 1974, working at store 14 in Upper Darby, Pennsylvania:

> *We used to have company baseball games in the field out back of Red Roof, one store playing against another. Grahame would always come out to the games. I had two children at the time. One was three and one was five and I had just gotten*

a divorce. I went to a game and I was sitting on the bench.
Grahame and his wife, Emilie were there, and he said to me,
"Why aren't you playing?"

I said, "I don't have a babysitter. My husband's gone,
you know."

"Well," he said, "I'll watch the kids."

And I said, "You will?"

And he said, "I will."

So he and his wife watched the kids while I played baseball
and when the game was over, he said, "We'll be here every
Tuesday." And they both came every Tuesday and watched my
kids. Emilie always brought a bag of goodies for the kids with
juice and treats. Isn't that awesome?

Grahame was "very humble," recalls Sal Mattera, who joined us as a twenty-one-year-old relief manager just out of the army and is still with us today, many decades later, as vice president of store operations. "You wouldn't know he was the CEO of Wawa if you met him on the street. He drove an old Ford Falcon station wagon until someone finally convinced him: 'Mr. Wood, you're the CEO. You have to get a new car.' But he was very frugal."

According to Sal, Grahame would notice "everything" when he dropped by his store in Lansdowne, Pennsylvania, on a surprise inspection:

Grahame was grading the store and he was taking what
seemed like forever to complete the grading. He seemed intensely
focused and I started to worry that something was wrong. Finally,
he came over to me and said, "I bet you thought your store was
perfect, but I took one point off because of dust in the back room
near a drain." Grahame wanted me to understand that there was
always room for improvement and that the smallest details of the

Thoughts on Managing the Business

(Dick Wood's column, *The Honker,* Wawa's company newsletter, 1986)

It is my job to create an environment under which each of us believes that we can make a difference. Recognizing the danger of controversy, the following is a laundry list of some of my random thoughts on the environment of the Company:

- Disdain for flash
- Education and training are encouraged
- Far better to make good long-term decisions even if they lead to painful short-term consequences
- No assigned parking spots or executive dining rooms
- Company's intelligence is in the front line—not in the executive suite; ideas should bubble to the top
- When in doubt, disclose information
- Don't tell others what to do . . . say why
- Preference for promoting from within
- Hard to know who's who in the pecking order
- Our company is more frenetic than others
- Our informal environment could drive others nuts
- Must hang on to energetic, enthusiastic habits
- Decisions should be made at the lowest possible level
- It's O.K. to make mistakes; progress is not possible without them
- We must remain vigilant to the "wants" of our customers
- We should strive to be the *best,* not the biggest
- The most important person in our company is the one ringing the cash register
- Our system may not work for others, but it does for us

If we each believe we can make a difference, we can achieve results that others would find impossible.

*business mattered most. A lesson learned that I have kept with me
over the years. If your glass was dirty, if you didn't have the right
signs up, things like that, he would correct it, but he would do it in a
nice way. He'd talk to you, coach you, and he spent time with you.*

Late in his life, when Grahame was very sick and near death, one of our real estate managers came into the store where store manager Al Madara was working, on Walnut Street in Philadelphia, and said, "Mr. Wood would like to see you."

"Where is he?" Al asked.

He was out in a van, lying down; he was that sick. But Grahame sat up to talk to his young store manager.

"Al," he said, "I just wanted to thank you for your years of service."

"It brought tears to my eyes," Al recalls.

It wasn't long after that that Grahame Wood knew for certain that his time on earth was nearly at an end.

He lay in bed in a hospital, thinking about his life and the brief time the doctors told him he had left.

"Emilie," he said to his wife, "I want to die at home."

An ambulance was soon called, and Grahame was wheeled into the vehicle for one last ride to his home in Wawa, Pennsylvania. Before the ambulance set out, however, Grahame had one last request.

"If you don't mind," he said to the driver, "would you be able to prop me up so I can see out the window? And could we go a few blocks out of the way? There's a store under construction on the corner of Twentieth and Tasker Avenue and I'd like to see how things are progressing."

That was Grahame Wood—to the very end.

Wawa grew quickly and, in 1978, Wawa opened its 200th store in Souderton, Pennsylvania.

CHAPTER 4

Learning to Fly

Of course, to anyone who's spent quality time in the Philadelphia region, the idea that Wawa is vastly more popular than any chain ought to be is familiar territory. But sometimes familiarity can create blindness to the big picture. For Wawa, the picture keeps getting bigger and bigger. Crazy customer loyalty has translated into eye-popping numbers and made Wawa one of the dominant economic forces in Philadelphia— one that supports an entire ecosystem of suppliers and vendors. And slowly—relentlessly—Wawa is transforming: altering its product mix, making bigger footprints whenever it moves.

—Don Steinberg, "It's a Wawa World," *Philadelphia Inquirer,* August 2011

Grahame Wood planted the seeds of an operation that his cousin Richard D. "Dick" Wood Jr. would grow into a company that could compete with the world's largest corporations.

Dick joined the board of directors of both the family textile operations in Millville and the dairy business in Wawa in 1965, as a twenty-seven-year-old

University of Virginia and University of Pennsylvania Law School graduate. A practicing attorney, Dick would later become Grahame's first general counsel in 1970. Before accepting a position with Wawa, Dick recommended the merger of the two businesses (Millville Manufacturing Company and Wawa Dairy Farms), enabling the company to utilize tax losses and cash from the sale of idle assets to fuel store growth. Like everyone else who ever worked at Red Roof, Dick first spent time on the front lines in Wawa stores, getting to know the daily challenges of the business and keeping customers satisfied and coming back.

"When I came to work at Wawa, everybody called him 'Mr. Wood,'" Dick says of his cousin Grahame. "I called him Uncle Grady, even though he wasn't my uncle. He was called Grady within the family because his father was called Grahame."

Dick would quickly start taking on more responsibility. He was a different kind of leader than Grahame. For one thing, Dick used to say that despite Grahame's military background, he tended to avoid difficult decisions. Dick himself had no problem in that regard. He quickly earned the respect of everyone in the organization for being decisive but fair. When Grahame brought in four outside directors to the board in 1973, they also supported Dick as a decision maker, and that gave Grahame even more confidence in his relatively young cousin.

In a short time, it became obvious that Grahame was grooming Dick to succeed him, though he never announced it formally. In 1977, a dozen years after first joining the company's board, Dick became Wawa's new CEO.

Transitioning company leadership between family members is not always smooth, or good for a company's long-term growth. Some CEOs in family companies have been known to select less qualified successors based on family ties, resulting in poor performance for years afterward.

This was not the case with Dick. He had every asset you could want in a leader, along with the same passion for the business that Grahame had. He was consistent, sought to build consensus, listened to diverse perspectives, and exhibited tremendous common sense—a quality that's much rarer in business than you might assume.

What also immediately stood out to people who met Dick was his informality and humility. Then a store manager, now vice president of store operations, Sal Mattera recalls:

> *Dick was such a down-to-earth guy. You wouldn't know*
> *he was president of the company if he was in your store. In*
> *many ways, [Grahame and Dick] were not that different.*
> *Dick was a little more outgoing than Grahame; he had a*
> *wonderfully dry sense of humor.*

Family members also describe Dick as a down-to-earth, humble man with a dry sense of humor. He drove a Honda stick shift for many years that he often parked next to the dumpsters behind Red Roof. On weekends in the winter he liked to split oak and hickory logs for firewood with his cousin, preferring to use a large maul that weighed over fourteen pounds. Though a blunt instrument, the maul was highly effective and suited Dick's stubborn determination to split even the knottiest of logs.

"He's humble to a point that he gets embarrassed," said Barbara Ennis, Dick's longtime executive office relationship manager. "If you tried to thank him for something, he would say, 'I didn't do it. I am surrounded by good people.'"

On November 17, 2000, Dick was honored with the Newcomen Society Award. Named for Thomas Newcomen, the great English inventor and entrepreneur, the society seeks to recognize people and institutions making positive contributions to the world around them and to celebrate the role of the free enterprise system in our global marketplace. At the ceremony, former

Pennsylvania governor and Philadelphia mayor Ed Rendell recalled another telling story about Dick:

> An organization is only as good as its leader and Dick is not only a good businessperson and a great corporate citizen, but he is an awesome individual. I don't know how many of you have had the experience of placing a call to Dick, but you will often get Dick on the phone. I don't mean through an assistant, I mean actually answering his own phone.
>
> I remember early in my administration as mayor of Philadelphia during one of our many crises, I had all of my staff assembled to handle some urgent problem and it was getting late in the afternoon. I knew that we were going to be there well into the night, so I called over to Dick's office hoping to get his secretary to see if they could help me order a six-foot hoagie to be delivered to the staff. I figured a Wawa hoagie would raise everyone's spirits, as well as feed them.
>
> Well, I didn't get the secretary, I got Dick—he actually answered the phone—so I was surprised, but told him why I was calling. I thought Dick would then graciously bump me to a general manager or direct me to a store, but no! Dick said, "There's no need, Ed, I can handle this. I don't think we can do a six-foot on such short notice because we have to order the rolls in advance, but how about three two-footers?"
>
> So I said, "Fine." And he proceeds to say, "What do you want on them?"

So here I am, talking to the CEO of a $2 billion-per-year company, placing a sandwich order. That story just goes to show what most of the people in this room already know—truly the type of extraordinary person Dick is.

I'm not exaggerating when I say that one of the toughest things I did as CEO was to convince Dick to put his signature on coffee cups. I urged him to do it because I knew people respected his name and liked Wawa's family heritage, but Dick was not comfortable with the exposure—that's the kind of unassuming man he is.

At the same time, Dick was seriously motivated and highly competitive. He hated to lose. That drive pushed him to oversee some of the most dramatic changes in Wawa's history, when it morphed into what millions of people have come to know as the Wawa brand today.

· · · · ·

Wawa was already a company in the midst of change when Dick took over.

Grahame's original strategy was that we would keep our doors open to sell groceries on Sundays and at night. Because the so-called blue laws then in force in most of the country wouldn't allow supermarkets to do the same, Wawa was one of the few, if only, places a customer could get a head of lettuce or a container of milk after 9:00 p.m. So Grahame's decision to carry perishables solved a basic problem for customers.

It was a successful business plan until 1972, when many supermarkets began expanding operations up to seven days a week. Simultaneously, big chains began to battle for market share through price cuts. That year was the first and only year the Wawa food markets suffered a financial loss. As a result, Wawa ceased store expansion and the company was forced to retrench.

By the end of 1973, the market stabilized, Wawa recovered, and we resumed expansion efforts. But it was the start of major changes in the company's identity.

When Pennsylvania's blue laws were officially thrown out by the state's supreme court in 1978, supermarkets could—and did—legally stay open around the clock, expanding their evening hours and operating seven days a week. Many installed service delis. As a result, Wawa lost much of what made it unique.

At that point, the company began to switch its strategy and instead targeted busy people on the go. That would start a series of interrelated changes. We began relocating stores to high-traffic areas, keeping our doors open twenty-four hours a day, providing more parking, carrying different products, and overhauling the customer experience. That's why, as I noted earlier, we no longer compete solely with supermarkets or convenience stores. We compete with Dunkin' Donuts, McDonald's, Starbucks, and ExxonMobil. As we like to say around Red Roof, "We run with the big dogs."

For people who have never been to a modern Wawaland, it is probably a little surprising how many stores we have in close proximity to one another. In some communities, we have stores as close as a mile apart. It's normal for many people to pass two, three, or four Wawa stores on a relatively short commute to work. This, in some ways, is our biggest and best form of advertising, because when the customer drives up and down every highway and they see a Wawa, it creates a bigger-than-life brand impression.

Obviously, we believe strongly in market dominance. In Greater Philadelphia, we have enough locations to compete against McDonald's. That's why we have chosen not to scatter and not to be in twenty states. It's better for us to be in six states and have all of our stores concentrated than spread out over half the United States.

We call this our cluster strategy. We figure if there's enough traffic, someone will put a store there—us or a competitor—so it might as well be us. The concentration enables us to build a more efficient infrastructure. Thanks to our relatively confined geographical area, we can achieve greater efficiency through fuel storage terminals and distribution centers that are able to get the product delivered to our stores in a more timely fashion.

The issue was clustering versus cannibalization. By clustering we give our units "sister stores" with which to share people, product, and customers. When one store runs out of coffee, it can get temporary replenishment from a sister store sometimes faster than with a warehouse delivery. Or if a customer needs something one store is out of inventory on, they can be referred to another Wawa a short walk or ride away. This provides significant economies of scale right down to the level of supervision of stores.

The cluster strategy also discourages competitors. Who wants to come in and build new convenience stores when there are already four hundred Wawa stores in a given geographic marketplace?

For this reason, we don't strive to be a national retailer. We don't want to saturate the entire East Coast. McDonald's may have twenty-two times as many stores as us nationally, but when you're in the Philadelphia marketplace, the perception of Wawa is bigger than that of McDonald's.

The result is that in Philadelphia almost three-quarters of all trips to convenience retailers are to a Wawa store. When it comes to products like coffee and breakfast sandwiches such as our Sizzli®, close to 25 percent of the products sold every morning in our hometown are at a Wawa store. On coffee alone, we go head-to-head with the national giants, and consistently have greater market share in Philadelphia. We have also surpassed ExxonMobil, Sunoco, and Hess for gas sales and market share in the Greater Philadelphia area. People in the industry said that couldn't be done, but Wawa did it anyway.

This success did not come easy. We've had our share of failures taking on the big dogs, including short-term disappointments that ultimately turned into successes. For example, we had a couple of stores with gas pumps in the 1970s and early '80s. But that early move into fuel was poorly thought out and not adequately supported by sophisticated equipment and canopies with adequate lighting, so we elected to stop expansion and remove tanks and pumps in 1982. Eleven years later, we tried again and succeeded.

Similarly, we tried to introduce built-to-order cappuccinos, lattes, and espressos in the early 1990s after seeing the specialty hot beverage trend become popular in Seattle. When we tried, though, it was a dud. We were more than a decade ahead of our time; the product concept had not been mainstreamed and our customers preferred the cappuccino out of our self-serve cappuccino machines, which had been in our stores for a few years. It was not until we introduced smoothies in 2011 that customers began to think of us for full-serve beverages. In 2012, we launched full-service espresso-based specialty beverages again, and this time the timing was right.

Other experiments we will probably never revisit, but we learned from them. We once served a stromboli (a kind of Italian turnover filled with cheese and meat), which we called a Wawa Boli®. It was wildly popular at first, but we could not get consistent quality on a large scale. We reluctantly had to abandon it, but that's the kind of move we have to make to ensure that we only serve the best products.

Occasionally, like every company, we make out-and-out mistakes. At one point, we thought Wawa should become the Trader Joe's of convenience stores. Our marketing team had a new person on board to help with this. He did a pretty good job with developing private-label products, but decided to change up our light-beige coffee cup and became obsessed with developing a new one. They tested many potential replacements, settled on one, put a new cup in production, and rolled it out to the stores.

There was just one problem. When you poured hot liquid into this cup, it created an aroma. An odor, actually. No, not an odor; that word doesn't really do it justice. It was a most awful stink! The cups were in circulation for two months before we identified a chemical in the black ink on the outside of the cups that exuded a terrible odor when hot coffee was poured into them. It didn't affect the taste of the coffee, but who wanted to drink from something that smelled so bad?

The issue came to a boil when Angelo Cataldi, a local personality on Sportsradio 610 WIP in Philadelphia, who enjoyed Wawa and stopped by one of our stores every morning for coffee, was accused by his co-workers— *on the air!*—of having an offensive body odor.

"It's not *me*, I swear!" he said. "It's this Wawa cup of *coffee!*"

Talk about a public relations nightmare. We had already discovered that the cups smelled, and as we were trying to quietly investigate and solve the problem, it was suddenly being discussed on a morning radio show heard by tens of thousands of Wawa fans and customers.

As you can imagine, the old coffee cups were back in our stores pretty darn fast after that. We even visited Angelo to apologize and present him with his own custom coffee mug.

Other initiatives remain dormant for years and years. We have joked for decades that we're still testing pizza. We've probably tried every pizza in the world, and we've never been able to find the right one for us. Will we stop testing? Probably not. It's a cultural desire that we not give up if we believe there's an opportunity to succeed with something eventually.

Unlike a lot of large corporations, we don't have a huge research and development facility, but we talk to our customers and stakeholders constantly. When we test new products, we are in the stores, listening to our consumers,

The Legend of Wawa Coffee

Throughout the six-state region we serve, Wawa's coffee is widely popular and known for its quality and variety. Since 2000, Wawa has served more than a billion cups of coffee and can claim a significant share of the brewed coffee market, ranking number one in Philadelphia and number seven nationally.

Wawa Coffee through the Years: In 1975, freshly brewed coffee became available in Wawa stores because store managers wanted to save busy customers time. When coffee was first introduced, pour-over pots were used. Stores soon had pots of water lined up in the morning rush to accommodate customers. In 1978, the coffee program "perked up" with the introduction of the five-burner Bunn-o-Matic, which accessed filtered water directly, allowing managers to make coffee with the flick of a switch.

In the 1990s, we remodeled and expanded the coffee areas to separate the brewing area from the customer area. The addition of the 20-ounce cup and later the Big 24 further fueled Wawa's coffee program. In 2010, Wawa embarked on a chainwide coffee makeover, completely transforming the coffee areas in all stores with new graphics, new designs, and energy-efficient thermals to replace glass pots.

Quality and Variety: Wawa's product development team, which includes coffee specialists, conducts sensory testing and develops specifications for our blends and roasts that produce the perfect cup of coffee for our customers. Wawa coffee is brewed fresh in stores using the most up-to-date equipment and systems in the industry. Coffee can be poured and prepared by customers to their preferences with a variety of flavorings.

Wawa is unrivaled in the number of coffee varieties we offer to please the palate of every customer. Our offerings include regular, decaf, and varietals, French vanilla, hazelnut, Colombian, and dark roast for those who prefer a stronger brew. The Wawa beverage line also includes hot, iced, and frozen built-to-order espresso-based specialty beverages. Our World Brew program features a rotation of blends and varietals from around the world.

listening to our store associates, finding out what's working, and just as eagerly discovering what's not. It was never destined that the Wawa of today would look and feel the way it does—that took planning, outside help, and some happenstance.

Take the story of associates such as Vic Musso, one of our early entrepreneurs. Like other managers, he would brew his own coffee at work. One day, one of his regular customers caught a whiff of the brew and said, "Boy, that coffee smells good."

"I've got plenty," Vic said. "Let me pour you a cup."

That simple exchange gave Vic and other Wawa associates the idea to sell coffee. Believe it or not, serving coffee was against company policy at the time, but when Grahame Wood saw how much customers enjoyed it, the policy changed.

Today, it's hard to imagine Wawa without our fresh-brewed coffee. In fact, there are countless fans who swear they wouldn't dream of starting a day without a cup of our special brew. It can all be traced back to the entrepreneurial spirit of our associates.

In the 1990s, Dick Wood challenged us to take the company to the next level. He inspired us to see things differently and to think bigger, including bigger stores. At that point, it wasn't obvious that bigger was better. Smaller locations were easier to open and meant lower costs. But looking at the economics and our strengths, we found that bigger was better, at least for Wawa.

In 1994, we opened our first really big store in Tinicum, Pennsylvania, near the Philadelphia International Airport. It was 5,600 square feet and had fifty parking places—huge for our industry at the time. We decided that size gave us presence, room for lots of customers and parking, room for equipment and storage, and room to change and grow. Every store we've built since has been a superstore.

That same attitude carried over to our decision to enter the fuel business. Dick Wood was on the board of QuikTrip and previously served on the board of Sheetz. Both companies sold fuel, and their profits per store day exceeded ours. Chester Cadieux, founder and CEO of QuikTrip, had always encouraged us to get into fuel. Chester said we had the best "inside offer" (that is, the best assortment of products for sale inside our stores), and fuel could allow us to satisfy even more of our customers' needs.

When we opened our first modern gas store in August 1996, in Millsboro, Delaware, we bet the farm that gasoline was going to be an important new strategic weapon for Wawa. We became a new age gas retailer in that we had big, well-lit, clean convenient sites, and we priced our product very competitively. We invested in technology called the Veeder-Root system that allows us to monitor our underground tanks and piping to ensure that we are not leaking fuel and degrading the environment, as well as maintaining real-time inventory measures and adding the capability to order additional fuel automatically. The system feeds data to our distributors who can monitor our fuel levels to ensure timely deliveries and prevent our stores from running dry.

The move into gas was a big gamble. We found ourselves wondering, If we build it, will they come? They did—with cars, boats, mobile homes. The lines circled the store, and we had arrived in the fuel business.

I always knew that if we were going to run with the big dogs, we had to be a big dog—but we didn't have to be on the leading edge to thrive. In fact, we're rarely the first to introduce a new product, process, or marketing concept. Sheetz had the touchscreen-ordering system first. We let them learn the tough lessons, then we borrowed the idea and improved on it. McDonald's did a great job of invention with the Egg McMuffin, but we mainstreamed the Wawa breakfast sandwich with the Sizzli® in 1996. Our success has been in adapting popular concepts, then making them available quickly and easily to our customers.

We also don't try to do everything ourselves. We specialize in building and operating stores, and rely on a great vendor structure. Our name may be on the door and people may associate all these products with Wawa, but if our vendors didn't invest in our business, we just wouldn't be as successful.

For example, Missa Bay, LLC was a produce distributor that started working with us more than forty years ago. The company had a small facility in the produce district of Philadelphia, located near the sports complexes that housed the Phillies, Eagles, '76ers, and Flyers. It distributed produce daily to our stores. The first time I met Frankie Pollera, Missa Bay's CEO, we sat in a cluttered, small back room with boxes of fresh produce everywhere, and we brainstormed.

That conversation led to Wawa offering fresh-daily green salads, cut fruit, and cut vegetables ready to be consumed, which grew into a booming business. It also led to the preparation of hot fresh foods, and development of a Wawa Fresh Channel and supply chain where items like fresh-cut fruits, salads, and bakery items are delivered daily, enabling us to get into the immediate-consumption food service business.

Another partner, J&J Snack Foods Corporation, runs our bakery. It is a dedicated plant that distributes products fresh every day exclusively through our stores. We also have a dedicated warehouse run by the McLane Company that distributes all of our tobacco, frozen items, refrigerated food service items, and dry products to our stores every other day. We have fuel storage tanks in the port of Wilmington, Delaware, that are operated by the Magellan Company. These are long-term partnerships.

About a decade ago, we needed to replace a retail software package that was fragmented and failed to give us fast, quality data. Frustrated, we tore out the guts of our existing legacy tech infrastructure in 2006 and put in a whole new system developed for us by SAP. That simple step—gigantic in the commitment and companywide buy-in it required—helped simplify and accelerate decision making across the organization because we had better, real-time information.

A quarter century ago we installed boil-in-bag technology in our stores. We didn't have kitchens, but the restaurant business was embracing this new technology. Products would come in frozen, and we'd put them in hot water, rethermalize them, and get a restaurant-quality product. Today a lot of restaurants are using boil-in-bag technology. It's another example of how, to compete with the best, we've had to work closely with vendor partners to deliver a unique experience.

Another one of our keys to success against competitors is our consistency. When we entered the convenience industry, 7-Eleven was already a national chain, but we found an advantage by making all our stores company owned and company operated. Other convenience store chains use a franchise model. That means they're not nearly as consistent as we are and have a much different corporate culture; and their corporate business has always been about selling franchises first, convenience second. Our business is about running each and every store on our own and maintaining consistency throughout the chain.

Essentially, we've become successful by both expanding our perspective and narrowing our playing field. We strive to be the best in the world at frequent, immediate, quick, and easy products. Before we realized that, we probably attempted to appeal to too many people and do too many things. Choosing our opportunities, staying true to who we are, staying true to the needs of our customers, and building the infrastructure—those are the things that help us run with the big dogs.

It may sound simple, but it wasn't easy getting here—and for that we have the pioneering leadership of Grahame and Dick Wood to thank.

Wawa has always been commitment to its associates. one of the many ways it shows this commitment is through the Employee Stock Ownership Plan (ESOP)—Wawa associates have a 38% ownership stake in the company.

CHAPTER 5

Private and Shared Ownership

Wawa employees often feel strongly that their success is closely tied to that of the company, in large part because employee stock ownership makes it their company too. Chuck Schlarp, 43, of Dennis Township and a general manager with 20 years at Wawa, said the company's employee stock ownership plan "ties us, more than cash compensation, not only to my store's performance, but also to helping out with my partners' stores. To me, that's huge. If they're doing poorly, it affects my financial future too.

—Kevin Post, *Press of Atlantic City,* May 20, 2012

In the last several chapters, you've read about how Wawa has changed over the years. But equally important are the things that have not changed. There are several unvarying elements of the Wawa way that are essential to who we are, that help make it possible for us to be the kind of people-centered business we are.

One of the most crucial of these elements is our ownership structure, which itself has two components: private ownership and the shared ownership among members of the founding family and company associates.

Being privately held rather than having Wawa shares traded publicly on the stock exchange allows us to take a personalized, long-term view of our company's future while always staying true to our core values. It allows us to make continued investments in new ideas, in our associates, and in our communities.

Private ownership is deeply embedded in our mentality and has always been part of the Wawa DNA. It gives fuel, life, and breath to our culture. That culture, celebrated as it is within and without, would be very, very different today if we were a Wall Street company. Private ownership—powerful and sustainable—is a deeply held belief not to be compromised at Wawa.

Years ago, when Wawa associates had an opportunity to buy stock in the company to keep us private, they did it. (I'll explain how that came about in some detail later in this chapter.) They were motivated by a desire to preserve the essence, the very fabric of the company, even more than by the belief that it would be a great financial investment, which it turned out to be.

Private ownership has a number of concrete benefits for Wawa. We don't have quarterly reports that must be submitted to Wall Street. The reports we generate are for internal communications, our associate owners, and key stakeholders. We're not making decisions, as a lot of companies do, based on what Wall Street analysts or minority investors will think. We're making decisions based on the best long-term interest of the business. Once a company goes public, it has no immunity to the whims of the markets and market investors. This leads to short-term decision making and a tendency to mortgage the future for the present. That can be intensely painful for organizations of all sizes.

We have always taken a long-term point of view about Wawa, no matter who is sitting in the CEO's seat. If an investment made sense long term, even if it required us to forego significant profits in one year for what we thought was right over multiple years, that's something we've always been willing to do.

Sometimes long-term thinking is reflected in little details. For example, we experienced a series of accidents in which customers put their foot on the gas rather than the brake in front of our stores, plowing right through the front windows and narrowly avoiding serious injuries to customers and associates inside. As a result, we decided to install concrete bollards (protective vertical posts) outside every single store. It was hard to justify in terms of return on investment, but in terms of living our values and protecting people, it was the right thing to do.

Another investment Wawa made that had no financial return was the move to armored car pickup for all of our store deposits. At the time, store managers were traveling to the bank to make the deposits themselves. Managers would often carry the cash deposits in brown paper bags to the bank, often on foot. The danger this presented to our associates was too great to bear and the $2 million cost of switching to armored cars was the right decision to protect our associates from danger. Safety was the driving factor. The fact that there was no immediate business return didn't matter.

We've always believed that steady, consistent growth is the cornerstone of our success. We've had private equity companies offer us money for an opportunity to take our brand nationally and expand a lot faster, but that's not something that drives us. What does drive Wawa is being the best we can be as a convenience retailer, continually raising the bar, and competing against ourselves to be better and better—not growth for the sake of growth.

. . . . .

The tradition of private ownership of Wawa began with its origins as a family business. Wawa has been the vehicle that literally keeps our founding Wood family together. Some family members have never sold stock in their individual trust because if they did then they'd no longer be part of something bigger than themselves. So it's much more than an investment; it's the glue that maintains and supports the traditions and values that have sustained the Wood family for years.

But private and shared ownership is more than just a way of keeping the Wood family involved with Wawa, valuable as that is. It's also a highly valuable tool for retaining associates, rewarding hard work and loyalty, and being nimble in an ever-changing marketplace.

Research gathered by the ESOP Association shows that companies with such plans enjoy much higher levels of associate engagement, tend to be especially stable and productive, and often become successful businesses.[3] Wawa offers powerful proof of this concept. Wawa's employee stock ownership plan (ESOP) is one of the top ten ESOPs nationally, in terms of number of participants. We believe that the combination of our private and shared ownership and our culture based on core values provide a competitive advantage that distinguishes us from other businesses and retailers.

---

3 For more information, please see www.esopassociation.org.

Private and Shared Ownership

Wawa's shared ownership philosophy started modestly decades ago and was dramatically expanded in the past decade. In 1992, the ESOP had 4,000 participants; by 2012, we had more than 9,500 participants. In 1992, the ESOP owned 8.3 percent of the company; by 2012, the ESOP owned 38.3 percent of the company. Today, Wawa's ESOP largely takes the place of a traditional retirement plan.

"The initial concept for having an ESOP at Wawa was Dick Wood's idea," Vince Anderson, former vice president and general counsel at Wawa, says. "Dick's ideas about profit sharing and sharing the ownership of the company were among the great, strong features that kept good people, rewarded them for good work, and ultimately proved to be very beneficial when they retired."

Here's how the ESOP program works. Once an associate has worked more than a thousand hours in a year and is over twenty-one years old, we contribute automatically to his or her ESOP account based on company profitability and his or her income during the year. This sum of money is used to allocate stock to the respective associate's ESOP account. And over time, that just builds and builds and builds. As the company grows—we've added a lot of eligible associates—participation in the ESOP grows as well.

Of course, there are trade-offs to being a partially ESOP-owned company. In most cases, ESOP companies tend to grow in a slower and more predictable fashion than other businesses. We don't strive to be a national retailer. Instead, we will continue to be a retailer with a few Wawalands clustered in carefully selected states and regions.

To us, the inability to access a broader capital pool as a private company is a small price to pay in exchange for controlling our own destiny. Our mission is to have a consistent store-level experience, in every Wawa, made possible in a private ownership structure. Capital often isn't the limitation on our new store growth. Rather, it's cultivating the right Wawa talent and assurance of transferring the Wawa culture to each new store. There are examples, when money is free in the public markets and growth is demanded by public shareholders of companies making poor decisions that lead to sloppy execution. Our commitment to private ownership, enables us to think long term and to grow at our pace while maintaining our culture.

To be privately held, you've got to be patient and you've got to persevere. But it also enables us to do things that Wall Street doesn't embrace. It enables Wawa to invest in the future.

We can spend almost $6 million on every new store—which is much more than our competitors invest—because we answer to ourselves rather than to Wall Street. Wall Street would choke over numbers of that nature. Expanding into Florida involved taking the risk of not making money in that new market for years to come. That's the kind of strategy Wall Street is not enamored of. But it works for Wawa.

Wall Street also doesn't like volatility. Yet profits in the gasoline business can be extremely volatile. We can have quarters when we fall behind budget and behind prior-year numbers, followed by quarters when just the opposite happens. We can roll with those punches, because we don't have to explain ourselves to "the Street."

Wall Street prefers companies to project quarterly and annual earnings. But if they fall short, they get hammered by the markets in terms of the stock price and negative press. Wawa has never wanted the focus to be on the price of its stock. We didn't want our associates to be preoccupied by daily gyrations in our stock price. We announce our revised stock price just once a year—and it's an exciting event. Some of our associates get together and log on to our company intranet to view the annual video announcement as soon as it's posted. They celebrate, then get back to business.

As this example suggests, the greatest impact of the ESOP may be on the relationship between Wawa and its associates. It's wonderful to have a job that you like, but it's even better to be able to share in the success of the company you work for. The harder and smarter our associates work, the more we all reap the benefits.

Here are some of our associates' thoughts on the ESOP, as told by Wawa associates during an ESOP Ownership Essay contest in 2012. "What does ownership mean to me?" wrote Peter Ricard.

> *"It means Wawa is part of our home. It's the pride that my son, who can't talk yet, knows that Wawa is the yellow goose on my shirt, on my jacket, on my beach towel, on my hat, and like many of you, nearly all my articles of clothing. He points to it when you ask him, "where's Wawa?" and smiles with recognition of a familiar icon . . .*
>
> *Ownership means this is "my home" and we don't leave a spill on the counter; you clean it up so the next person doesn't have to. Ownership is knowing that your friends and neighbors trust you, are your family, and we come together at Wawa, even on a Saturday morning when you look a mess.*

For the eight years that I was the CEO of Wawa, I loved the fact that I worked for our associates and served them day in and day out. "I truly work for you," I told them on many occasions, "because you are the owners of this company." As a result, they know it's their business.

Our people have always felt an emotional connection to the business, but what really empowers our store teams and our associates is the emotional connection coupled with the financial connection of the ESOP. One without the other wouldn't be nearly so powerful.

. . . . .

Dick Wood was the champion of the Wawa employee stock ownership plan. Time and time again throughout our history, he proved himself to be passionate about private ownership and shared ownership, demonstrating the courage and conviction to block attempts to go public or take private equity from outside investors.

Today, because of Dick's conviction and dedication to these principles, our private ownership stands solidified, but it took a lot of work and negotiation to keep it that way.

When Dick took the reins of the company, all of the descendants of George Wood were beneficiaries of the 1922 Trust, while George Wood's two daughters and their descendants were beneficiaries of the 1923 George Wood Trust. The 1922 Trust and 1923 Trust owned, respectively, 41 percent and 25 percent of Wawa's shares. Both trusts shared the same trustees, one of which was Fidelity Bank.

Ownership in a private company is an anathema for a corporate trustee (such as Fidelity) because if the company does well, the corporate trustee gets no credit and if it craters, the corporate trustee worries that it will be held responsible for a surcharge by the beneficiaries.

The odd paradox is that the better Wawa performed, the greater Fidelity Bank's apprehension grew.[4] In 1988, at Fidelity's insistence, an effort was made to diversify the two trusts. This effort became mired in the Orphan's Court of Delaware County, the legal jurisdiction of the two trusts, until finally the diversification effort was aborted in 1991.

Recognizing his personal conflict of interest during the diversification effort, Dick subsequently visited Orphan's Court judge Francis J. Catania and asked to be relieved as a trustee. He then asked the judge to appoint

4   In 1994, Fidelity successfully filed a petition to resign as trustee.

one family member from each of the four branches of George Wood's descendants to serve along with Fidelity Bank. Dick's effort to ensure equity among the family branches proved to be a decision he would regret, as the family trustees subsequently made requests to take the company public.

In addition, an investment advisor to the family trustees continually—to Dick's great frustration—recommended that the company either be sold or that the trusts be diversified through a public offering.

In a 1996 letter, legal counsel to the trusts was directed by one of the trustees "to line up ten possible buyers and to be prepared to talk about an initial public offering at the next trust meeting." In an effort to thwart this course of action, which he knew would lead to the sale of Wawa, Dick wrote a memorandum to the Wawa board of directors criticizing the action. As a result, a special committee of the board's independent directors was formed to provide the trustees with an analysis of the company's prospects for future performance. In a report dated March 27, 1997, the special committee recommended that the trusts maintain their holdings in Wawa.

This action and recommendation did little to appease the trustees, the investment advisor, or their counsel, as they continued to pursue either a sale of the company or a public offering. Finally, in 1998, to stop a sale of the majority ownership, Dick recommended that the 1923 Trust's 25 percent interest be sold. Several private equity firms were consulted by Dick and Wawa chief financial officer Ed Chambers (1988–2000). In April 1998, two of these firms bid against each other and the 25 percent interest was sold for $525 a share, or a total of $83.8 million. The equity partner received two important commitments from the company in conjunction with the sale: First, the equity partner received a right to demand that Wawa make a public offering of its stock five years after the transaction took place in May 1998; and second, they placed two directors on the Wawa board.

As a result, Wawa board meetings took on a rather dysfunctional tone.

When the proscribed five years had passed, in 2003, the equity partner made it evident that it would exercise its demand registration rights; in other words, it called for Wawa to become a publicly traded company. To this end, in the spring of that year, the company and the equity partner interviewed four Wall Street investment banks and selected two of them to take Wawa public in an IPO to be held in the fall, although a decision was made to hold off the major documentation until after the company's second-quarter earnings were available.

In July 2003, the two investment banks came to Red Roof with an entourage of more than a dozen representatives and met with several members of Wawa's management team. Investment bankers, who always bring books with pages of detailed financial information to such meetings, droned through a litany of recent public offerings that had gone to market in the first half of 2003, to demonstrate recent market performance and its potential impact on Wawa's value.

As they did, Dick flicked to the back of the book and did a back-of-the-envelope calculation on their proposed price for the company in the public offering. It was 35 percent *less* than the price the firms had estimated just three months earlier. When this price was confirmed by the entourage from the two investment firms, they were quick to point out that the IPO market had "tanked" in the interim three months.

Dick said that Wawa and its equity partner had no interest in a public offering at such a reduced value.

The room became deathly silent.

Dick was the first to speak.

"I feel like a skunk at a picnic," he said.

Everyone laughed, stood up, shook hands, and parted ways. That was the closest Wawa ever came to being publicly owned.

Subsequently, negotiations took place between the equity partner and Wawa to purchase the firm's shares using a combination of Wawa cash and funds from the company's employee stock ownership plan.

Two major events spurred this: First, Wawa was introduced to the concept of company associates transferring funds, tax free, from their personal 401(k) and profit-sharing accounts to their ESOP accounts; second, negotiations took place with the equity partner to have the company acquire its shares for $888.98 per share, or $142 million—a win-win for both parties as the partner received a fair return on its initial investment and Wawa was able to remain private.

The company now had an opportunity to turn lemons into lemonade. To make this happen, Wawa associates needed to voluntarily transfer sufficient funds to their ESOP accounts to supplement the company's funds, and to permit the acquisition of the shares at the negotiated price.

On December 3, 2003, Dick announced the intention to purchase the equity partner's 25 percent ownership interest:

> *To help fund the purchase, the Company's ESOP will be offered the opportunity to participate in the purchase of some of these shares. The Company's associates will be given the opportunity to transfer a portion of their existing Savings and Profit Sharing accounts to the ESOP and the ESOP will use those transferred amounts to fund the purchase . . .*
>
> *I am excited about the prospect of continuing to grow the portion of Company shares owned by our associates through the ESOP. As I said in my earlier letter, it will strengthen the bond between the Wood family and employee*

ownership of the Company—a bond I believe has been fundamental to our core values and our past success . . .

The past few years have exposed corporate transgressions at some of our nation's largest public companies, from Enron to Worldcom. These companies are the opposite of what we have at Wawa. There, the short-term pressures of Wall Street corrupted executives. That is not the case here at Wawa. Your management is firmly behind this transaction. You can rest assured that we all have committed to transferring our profit sharing and 401k savings into the ESOP with confidence. From a personal point of view, we also have a lot to gain or lose from this transaction. We wouldn't have it any other way.

My goal has always been that Wawa remains privately held. It's my firm belief that better-run companies have an ESOP. I have sat on the boards of QuikTrip and Sheetz, both of which have combined an ESOP with family ownership. This has been an underpinning of their success.

Making the long-term focus a priority is not a new idea at Wawa. Twenty years ago, I published a document describing our culture as one of teamwork, everyone making a difference, long-term focus, consensus and an informal environment that would, perhaps, drive others nuts. This has all been driven by the ownership of the company. Today, those beliefs remain the same. And we believe that these beliefs have driven our success. With the success of the ESOP option, we can and will continue to put those beliefs into practice.

Making an offering to expand employee ownership was, in many ways, similar to the process of taking Wawa public. We filed registration papers and made a formal offering to our associates. We organized a road show to tell our story to associates, presented the options, and let Wawa associates make their own decisions.

Dick Wood, Thère DuPont (our chief financial officer at the time), and I traveled to the five states where Wawa operated, held employee meetings, and encouraged spouses to participate in those meetings. We laid out what we were doing, what the options were, and made it as clear as possible that participation was purely voluntary. These were their funds, not ours, and opting in was entirely up to them.

Of course, we couldn't promise financial results for the future. If the associates looked at our financial results for the twenty years preceding that offering, they saw that we had done well compared to Wall Street indices. But you can never assume that will continue, so we presented our case just as any company that goes public would.

It's important to note that this was a one-time offer, with a deadline. Associates had to decide to opt in by March 5, 2004. Of our eligible participants in 2003, 70 percent accepted the offer and transferred some or all of their savings or profit-sharing balances into the ESOP. Our need was to raise a minimum of $45 million from our associates, an amount required to supplement the company's funds in order to repurchase the shares from the equity partner. Even with an investment of this size by the associates, our growth plans would be negatively impacted for several years to come. In line with this, we announced our plans to hold the line on major expenditures for at least two years.

That turned out to not be a problem, as the offering was actually oversubscribed. Associates elected to invest $59 million in their company, far in excess of our wildest dreams. It was an extraordinary vote of confidence in the company from the people who knew it best.

In my mind, it was a vote from the heart more than a financial decision, but it turned out to be a tremendous financial decision for everyone as well. Those who bought in did phenomenally well. Their support sustained the company and solidified private ownership of Wawa. It was a defining moment in the history of our company.

Today, Wawa associates own more than 38 percent of the company through the ESOP. The associates who participated in the historic transaction turned the sale of the 1923 Trust from a lemon to lemonade.

· · · · ·

There was another matter relating to the ownership of Wawa that Dick needed to address to ensure the private ownership status for the future.

When a trust breaks up, those responsible for it, the trustees, distribute the financial assets in accordance with the terms of the trust document. The 1922 George Wood Trust still owned a controlling interest in Wawa. Scheduled to break up in 2030, this represented a huge ownership cliff. By then, the value of the company might be so significant as to make it impossible for our associate ESOP to buy the trust shares.

To avoid this problem, Dick went to the Wood family in 2011, and the courts, and said, "Let's take the trust and divide it into thirty-eight separate trusts by income beneficiary (or family head) giving control of that family's proportionate number of trust shares to that family. Then, let each of the income beneficiaries of the George Wood Trust control their own trust shares through being their own trustee, and make their own decisions about diversifying their

ESOP Fast Facts

Wawa's culture is based on private ownership, shared ownership, and a commitment to living our core values. Our unique ownership structure is comprised of descendants of the founding family and employees, through the company's ESOP. Here is a concise history of its evolution:

- 1977: Wawa began its commitment to sharing ownership with associates by forming the company's original profit-sharing plan.
- 1992: Profit-sharing plan shares were transferred to an ESOP formed by Wawa.
- 1992: The ESOP had approximately **4,000** participants, who owned 8 percent of the company.
- 2004: Associates purchased shares of a non-family investor enabling the company to remain private and increase employee ownership to 27 percent.
- 2009: Wawa celebrated National Employee Ownership Month with activities to celebrate our associate owners.
- 2012: Wawa distributed name tags bearing the slogan proudly associate owned to celebrate the company's ownership culture with the community.
- 2013: Wawa's ESOP grew to more than **9,500** participants, who owned 38 percent of the company.

Based on statistics from the ESOP Association, the number of employee participants **ranks Wawa's ESOP in the top ten** in the United States.

individual trust accounts. If they want to diversify their holdings in Wawa stock, this will give them the ability to do so. That way, they don't need to have all their apples in one basket unless they choose that option."

The court ruled in favor of Dick's plan after all 107 family members over the age of eighteen signed the petition to the Orphan's Court. As a result, the beneficiaries of the subtrusts now have the opportunity, once a year, to tender Wawa stock back to the company or to the ESOP and then reinvest those funds however they choose. The decision presents an opportunity for Wawa to sustain private ownership for the next fifty to a hundred years. Many of us in leadership today won't be around then, but this was something that, at Wawa, we talked and thought a great deal about.

This is different than what people in public companies contemplate. They're not thinking about fifty to a hundred years out. We at Wawa already have two hundred years behind us, so we look far ahead. It's an approach to business that has served us pretty well so far, and we hope it will continue to do so for centuries to come.

As you can see, our private ownership status was at risk several times during our history. Dick Wood's personal courage and strong conviction to remaining private, aligning stakeholders, and sharing ownership with associates was a defining time in our first fifty years. These key moments, when Dick stood tall, created a wonderful opportunity to stabilize ownership and for associates to share in Wawa's success for generations to come.

At Wawa, being a leader requires a passion for serving your fellow associates.

CHAPTER 6

Servant Leadership

Leadership is both an art and a science. Everyone is the leader and everyone can also be a servant.

—Robert Greenleaf, *The Servant as Leader*

Private ownership and shared ownership are key parts of the moral compass that keeps Wawa on course. The third part of this compass is something called servant leadership.

If you've worked for a variety of companies in your career, you know that most are managed from the top down. The executives make all the key decisions, consulting only their own perspectives and often with their own best interests at heart. Everyone else affected by those decisions, including employees, customers, and the communities in which the companies operate, simply have to accept those decisions and make the best of them.

Wawa is quite different in this regard. We exist to serve our friends, neighbors, and communities, and to serve our 21,000 associates so they can serve our customers. Rather than a top-down organization, Wawa is a bottom-up organization. We empower our associates to do the wonderful things that make this company great. This, in a nutshell, is the concept of servant leadership—one in which the executives are called to serve, support, and nurture the associates. It inverts the traditional corporate hierarchy, placing the leaders at the bottom of the organizational chart and the associates at the top. The servant leadership model was named and defined by Robert Greenleaf half a century ago when he wrote his classic book, *The Servant as Leader*. It "begins with the natural feeling that one wants to serve, to serve first," Greenleaf explains.

Here is how C. Williams Pollard, Chairman of Service Master, described such leaders in the publication *The Leader Who Serves*.

The real leader is not the person with the most distinguished title, the highest pay or the longest tenure. The real leader is the role model, the risk taker. The real leader is not the person with the largest car or the biggest home, but the servant. Not the person who promotes himself or herself, but the promoter of others. Not the administrator, but the initiator. Not the taker, but the giver. Not the talker, but the listener. Servant leaders believe in people they lead and are always ready to be surprised by their potential. Servant leaders make themselves available. Servant leaders are committed. They're not simply holders of position. They love and care for the people they lead. Leadership is both an art and a science. Everyone is the leader and everyone can also be a servant.

Grahame Wood and Dick Wood each embraced the spirit and the principles of servant leadership without calling it such. There are an endless array of stories about Grahame Wood picking up trash at the stores, speaking to each and every associate in the stores, inquiring with genuine interest about their families and their lives. If an associate had a need, Grahame did his best to help that associate out. He was empathetic; he was caring. When the dairy went through tough times, he opened the convenience store business to preserve jobs. All these actions reflect bedrock principles of servant leadership.

Dick Wood, in particular, is the epitome of servant leadership. Dick always talks about how the most important person in the company is the one ringing the register. His humility, his empathy, and his willingness to listen to people and demand that they be treated with dignity and respect made all the difference in the world in our company and our culture.

As his successor, I never tried to be Dick. I just tried, as Dick did, to preserve the things that Grahame Wood stood for. I've been nicknamed "The Storyteller" because that's what I spent my entire twenty-five years at Wawa doing: crafting the company story, building programs to support the story, and nurturing and manifesting the meaning of that story so it could be sustained over a long period of time. Great companies can lose their way over the years as the business is handed from generation to generation. Dick and Grahame embodied servant leadership to such a great degree that I felt it was incumbent upon me to pass the same tradition on to the next generation of Wawa associates. I wanted to feel confident that in thirty, sixty, or even ninety years, leaders at Wawa will still embrace those principles.

My own background reinforced the value of the servant leadership mindset. I spent twenty-five years of my career in human resources. And when you're in HR and you're hiring, training, career-pathing people, and making sure they're engaged, you focus on them. You focus on building their careers, and you don't worry about your own career. As a result, it became somewhat ingrained in me that my job was to build others' expectations and help them achieve success. Through their success, I would also achieve success.

One of the things I proposed on my very first day on the job as Wawa's new head of HR in 1987 was to discourage the use of the word *employee*. From that point on, we said *associate* instead—a word that I believe enhances the dignity and importance of every individual who works alongside us at Wawa. Maybe the choice of words we use seems like a small thing to worry about. But at Wawa we try to embody servant leadership in everything we do. Our corporate offices at Red Roof are humble, down-to-earth, even homey. The CEO of Wawa occupies a space that's incredibly modest compared to what you'd find in most companies. We think that's the way it ought to be.

Our management committee is also committed to the concept of servant leadership and to ensuring it continues well into our future, so much so that we have worked with St. Joseph's University, a Jesuit institution in Philadelphia, to tailor a program in which we could teach servant leadership. The program captures and shares the principles of servant leadership with the objective that it start with all Wawa leaders, from the management committee through the store manager level to the associates who will be store managers in the future. It is an extensive program in terms of what it means to be a servant leader. It then goes further to ensure that our performance appraisal and recognition programs also embody the principles of servant leadership.

Wawa isn't the only company to espouse servant leadership. Southwest Airlines is another, and they do it within a union environment, which is extremely challenging. But there are few companies that try to practice servant leadership as consistently as we do at Wawa. At Wawa, leadership is earned each and every day. It's a privilege, an honor bestowed upon you by those you serve, not necessarily by those you report to.

Of course, it's one thing to talk about servant leadership. Practicing it is much more challenging—and much more important. Servant leadership must be embedded in our culture. If we don't teach it, preach it, celebrate it, wrap our arms around it, and build institutions that embody it, it will dissipate and ultimately be forgotten.

The seriousness with which we take the servant leadership concept is reflected in the fact that when people are asked to leave Wawa, it's usually not for incompetence but rather because they didn't embrace servant leadership. They may tend to manage from the top down rather than from the bottom up; they may not be great listeners; they may not be empathetic; they may not engage their people. Whatever the specific problem, the result is that people don't want to be led by them.

We engage our associates in regular surveys to see whether our leaders are true servant leaders. When our leaders come up short, there are generally symptoms such as high turnover, complaints, grievances, and lower productivity. These are signs that our culture is rejecting them, the way the human body rejects outside organisms that don't belong.

There were several cases where the culture didn't rally around up-and-coming corporate leaders. The culture didn't embrace them. And it became obvious to everyone around the business and to the individual involved that it wasn't quite the right fit. I'm not sure that would happen in other companies. But at Wawa people feel empowered, and they speak up.

One of the main reasons we're writing this book is to pass along our special culture to future Wawa associates. We hope that putting these lessons in writing will help us hold tomorrow's leaders accountable.

Fortunately, at Wawa we have many positive examples of servant leadership to point to and learn from. One is Harry McHugh, our long-serving vice president of operations. Harry came to this country from Ireland, bringing with him great respect for the American tradition of free enterprise. Harry sent out a memo years ago thanking people for an incredible effort during a snowstorm, and signed the letter "Your humble servant."

Virginia Darby is the general store manager of the Wawa in Pittman, New Jersey. She told us that what makes Wawa's culture unique is the servant leadership displayed throughout the organization from every single level, beginning with the way we help our associates find their personal vision and then strive to make it a reality.

"It's the way servant leaders work alongside of us," she says. *"The way they spread out the credit to everybody and never take it for themselves; the way that they are approachable and adaptable and they'll do everything we do. I recognize that and that makes me so proud to work for a company like this.*

"I believe in servant leadership," Virginia adds. "I feel like whatever level I'm at, they're no higher or better. They're willing to get dirty alongside of me, help me do everything I need to do. They lead by example. They're the person that doesn't make me feel like I'm any different of a person. I'm right up there with them, from the CFO and the CEO to store operations. We're all in the same peer level. That's what servant leadership means to me."

. . . . . .

The Associates in Need program is one of Wawa's greatest manifestations of servant leadership. It's a wonderful idea that originated when we benchmarked ourselves against Southwest Airlines, which we've already mentioned as one of America's few corporations that has whole-heartedly embraced the idea of servant leadership.

For years, we wanted to study Southwest Airlines' corporate culture and see what we could learn from it to apply to Wawa. However, because of Southwest's unique culture and its highly successful track record of business results, the time and energy of its corporate leaders is very much in demand.

To get their attention, we sent Colleen Barrett, then the president of Southwest, a big milk crate full of our own private-label peanuts. I attached a note saying, "Our nuts are better than yours." (Southwest not only hands out bags of nuts on its flights but it also identifies with the idea of being "nuts" as part of its corporate identity; in fact, the classic book about Southwest's culture, by Kevin and Jackie Freiberg, is titled, simply, *Nuts!*)

Puzzled, Barrett called a colleague who said, "My sister lives in Virginia. Let me find out who this Wawa group is."

The sister said, "We love Wawa. We go there all the time."

As a result, we got an audience with Southwest and had the opportunity to benchmark ourselves against one of America's most admired companies.

The element that really intrigued us at Southwest was the airline's Employee Catastrophic Fund program. Employees contribute to a rainy-day charitable fund to help fellow employees deal with financial emergencies. We thought this sounded like a great way to formalize our long-standing custom of helping our people during tough times, which led to the creation of the Wawa Associates in Need Fund, a nonprofit 501(c)(3) charitable entity, which works in conjunction with our internal care department.

Wawa, along with Wood family members, provided seed money for the fund—a couple of hundred thousand dollars. (Both continue to contribute annually.) Then we invited associates to make tax-deductible contributions to the fund through payroll deduction.

It's evolved into a hugely successful program. More than 50 percent of Wawa associates contribute to the program, and it has grown from helping forty-seven associates that first year (2008) to more than five hundred in 2012. The program helps associates struck by natural disasters, catastrophic illnesses, spousal lay-offs, or other unexpected problems. It gets their heat turned back on in the middle of the winter, or provides the money needed to bury a loved one after a sudden death.

We're very thorough in researching an associate's circumstances to make sure the need is real; we require a lot of documentation and backup. But it is really great for our people to know that they have somewhere to turn in an emergency.

The Associates in Need Fund was one of the most rewarding things I saw accomplished at Wawa during my tenure. It surpassed our expectations and truly became a manifestation of serving others and making a difference in their lives.

Our internal care team, led by Barbara Ennis, has an extended mandate to be involved in associates' lives in many other ways, doing everything from sending birthday, wedding, first home, and graduation cards—up to four hundred cards a month—to baby gifts when an associate becomes a new parent. There is an Adopt-a-Family program every Thanksgiving in which we help out 225 families with ten days' worth of groceries, including a turkey and all the trimmings. We often send food trays or beverages when there is a death in the family. If an associate is recovering from surgery, we send Wawa blankets to comfort them.

Through actions like these, we try to send the message that Wawa associates and the communities they serve aren't just business connections to us. They are part of our family and deserve the kind of loving, personal support family members naturally receive.

Shared private ownership and servant leadership form the inner core of our success. Strip away any one of these elements and you'd strip away something vital from Wawa. The result would be less growth and less success. That's why we're committed to these ideas as key ingredients in the Wawa way.

Wawa's six core values define its culture and serve as the company's guiding light every day.

CHAPTER 7

Our Six Core Values

Wawa is a lifesaver to . . . emergency personnel and workers. Coffee, hot food, water, bathroom breaks, gas, all help the police, fire, EMS workers, township officials, public works, utility workers, and the press to do their jobs. I'm sure many Wawa workers would have preferred to stay home with their families or keep an eye on their homes during the storm, but instead, they were serving us and helping us to do our jobs. I stopped at a Wawa numerous times during my storm coverage and I couldn't have been happier to see that goose, bright and glowing, through the dark and rainy skies, each time.

—Courtney Elko, *Media Patch*,
November 1, 2012

Our moral compass of private ownership, shared ownership, and servant leadership keeps Wawa grounded. It ensures that we'll never behave in ways that compromise our concern for people or turn Wawa into a company that we're not proud of.

But, of course, it takes more than just a compass to find your way in the complex, challenging journey across today's business landscape. It also takes a road map—one that defines where you want to go as a company and the general path you plan to take to get there. Therefore we supplement our moral compass with a set of six company values that define us and serve as a kind of road map that guides our daily behaviors.

These six values are essentially the Wawa owner's manual:

Value People

Delight Customers

Embrace Change

Do Things Right

Do the Right Thing

Have a Passion for Winning

It wasn't until the 1990s that we clearly defined and identified these six values. We were aided in the process by a series of focus groups with our associates. They helped us get our hands around the values so that we could articulate them in language that everyone could understand and embrace.

In difficult times, we look at the Wawa values and ask ourselves what they indicate we should do in any given situation. The decisions we make must enhance and support most of the values without hurting the values they don't support. If a decision is aligned with the values, then it's a good decision. The values keep the company on course and help us discern right from wrong.

We probably spend more time than most companies defining, communicating, and measuring the values. We like to get down into the organization and tell stories about our people, how they bring these values to life and how they shape these values. If there was one accomplishment I was most proud of during my time as a leader at Wawa, whether it was as the head of human resources, marketing, or as CEO, it was nurturing and manifesting the company's values. These six values are our competitive advantage.

If people don't live the values, they won't survive at Wawa. In fact, people who don't buy into the values aren't likely to ever be hired. My predecessor, Dick Wood, and I personally met with every new associate hired at our Red Roof headquarters. We'd ask him or her to talk about their background and why they came to apply for employment at Wawa. Of course, their backgrounds and experience were very diverse. But they all shared the same values we talked about and reinforced at Wawa.

I remember one applicant saying, "I stalked your company for three to four years just waiting for a job to open up. I wanted to work for Wawa because of your value system." It's not the kind of comment you hear from job applicants at most companies, but at Wawa it's fairly typical.

Once new people come on board, it's up to us to train them and inculcate our values from day one. One way we do this is by honoring role models. Every year, we recognize more than three thousand associates who have done wonderful things to bring the core values to life. At every meeting we have, we talk about the core values. They are mainstreamed into the performance appraisal process. When we do 360-degree evaluations on leaders of the business and get feedback from the people they work with, core values are an important part of that. When we train people in leadership competencies, the core values are embedded in that, too. They're much more than words in a consultant's report on a bookshelf. They truly are how we live and build our business every day.

The world we live in may change, strategies may change, and goals may change. But the underlying essence of the business, our DNA, doesn't change. While we come together each year to refine and adjust our strategies, the core values are something we don't adjust. They're rock solid.

VALUE PEOPLE

Wawa associates are our number one competitive edge in a crowded marketplace. We are a people-intense business, dependent on 21,000 associates delivering the Wawa brand experience some 500 million times a year. So if we have great people, then we will have great customer relations—and that will bring us success at every level. That means that building people and building teams are keys to building our business.

How do we value people?

It starts with making sure their needs are being met. Compensation, benefits, and economic security are all important contributions to valuing people, and we need to make sure people are paid fairly, that they're properly incentivized, that they have benefits that protect them in times of illness or disability, and that they have a well-funded and attractive ESOP program.

But we also want to create an environment that empowers people to see their dreams come true, where they can be themselves, and where they want to come to work every day. Everyone wants his or her job to be more than just a job. And we want them to enjoy doing the work they do. We want them to know they contribute in a positive way to the community. We want them to realize that they make a difference.

As part of our effort to create a people-friendly environment, we work hard to treat each associate with dignity and respect by creating a team-based system rather than an individual-based system. We believe that teams win. Individuals have to be members of the team, and our systems of performance, recognition, and compensation are based on that.

We also create family environments within our work units. Each store is a microcosm of a family: three generations that come together to work three eight-hour shifts a day, serving their friends and neighbors. That's a wonderful situation. And they do it and have fun because we value each and every one of them.

We provide a flexible work environment that promotes a balanced lifestyle. We continuously invest in our people to support lifelong learning and self-development and to maintain a leadership position in our industry. We also practice safety first. We demonstrate care and respect for each other, our customers, and vendors. We are positive and optimistic; we believe that by working as a team, we can overcome any challenge and reach any goal.

Finally, we work hard and celebrate our successes, knowing that a bit of laughter is a valuable motivating force in the life of any individual. Fun is good business.

Building a people-friendly business starts with choosing the right people in the first place. In fact, Wawa manager Don Toogood says that the hardest part of his job is finding people who will be a good fit for his team.

"What I do sometimes is have current associates sit in on interviews to see how they feel about a prospective hire," he explains. "The opinion of an associate counts because they're the ones that have been with us already. If they have a strong feeling about somebody, good or bad, it can help us make a better decision."

Don says the team in his store can be described in two words: positive attitude.

"They all want to come to work; they want to do well," he says. "They want to see me succeed because I want to see them succeed. I spend time with them. I allow them to ask me any question at any time. And I'll stay late if I have to, to make sure they get the answers they need. I've been with my assistant general manager for a year, and we actually go to school together. We talk outside of work; we both have families. She just bought her first house."

Don Toogood exemplifies the kind of people-centered leadership we cherish. By building a great team, Don helps make it possible for all of us to succeed together—which is how we roll at Wawa.

DELIGHT CUSTOMERS

We never forget that customers have more choices today than they've ever had before.

There was a time when convenience stores had a unique and unchallenged niche in the retail landscape. Few other stores were open twenty-four hours a day. Supermarkets, drug stores, and fast-food places were closed most evenings and some weekend days. That created a clearly defined opportunity for convenience stores to seize.

In the modern era, however, there has been a blurring of retail channels; everyone is selling convenience today. That means everyone is trying to attract the same customer, which makes our job much harder than in the past.

In this tough new environment, our goal is to ensure a consistent customer experience that delivers high quality, reliable products and services at a competitive price. To become the preferred choice of our customers, we have to delight them, day in and day out.

The question is how. How do we stand above the crowd?

One of Wawa's earliest positioning statements actually came from a customer: "We do it just a little bit better." We're a company that tries not to boast; we do so many things, and we simply want to do them all a little bit better in the minds of the consumer. Even though that phrase is no longer our formal marketing position, what we said almost thirty years ago is still what we're known for today.

Of course, as the years have passed, our business has continually evolved. We are constantly looking for new, high-quality products that are consistent with our brand and that can contribute to our effort to delight our customers.

We will always carry national brands, but we want more and more of our products to be Wawa branded. We want to be known for high-quality, value-priced products the consumer can depend on, including a high percentage of our own products because they're special and highly regarded by our customers. There's only one place to get Wawa coffee, a Wawa hoagie, and Wawa milk, and that's at Wawa. Then we complement our brands with local and national brands that represent products we don't think we can match or beat.

Speed and ease of transactions are another big key to delighting our customers. We are a convenience retailer and we know customers don't want to go on a treasure hunt. They give us four or five minutes to get in and out of the store, satisfying whatever need drove them to us in the first place. To make it easy, our products are consistently located from store to store. We try to price consistently as well. Some retailers will market promotions that are available at certain locations but not others. We've never done that.

That said, if we don't introduce new concepts from time to time, we can't increase the frequency of our customers' visits. There's a fine line between protecting what the customers cherish yet giving them another reason to come back. Managing change and introducing new products while maintaining a consistent brand image is both art and science.

We were concerned when we went into the gas business because we still wanted to delight those customers who came to us for food. We didn't want gas to be a distraction. So we planned accordingly. We built bigger gas facilities specifically so they wouldn't interfere with the stores' other operations. Where most gas retailers have big, heavy canopies, we erred on the side of light, airy canopies—almost like wings on an airplane—because we wanted customers, as they drove down the highway, to see the attractive Wawa store as well as the gas outlet. Having a clear, consistent image that makes it easy for people to understand what we have to offer is an aspect of delighting customers.

Another element in our customer-delighting proposition is the customers themselves. Wawa, the Cheers of convenience stores, is a bit like the old general store: a place where people from the community come together to add a positive note to their day. Shopping at Wawa isn't just a sales transaction—it's a feel-good experience based on person-to-person interactions. Wawa is a place where customers hold doors open for each other. It's a place where strangers become friends—and sometimes much more.

We got a letter once from a customer saying that for months another customer whom she'd never met paid for her coffee every morning. Eventually they got to know one another, and he ended up becoming her husband. That's a great example of the Wawa mystique in action.

On October 6, 2007, Carol Bryant Jackson published a guest column in the *Delaware County Daily Times* under the headline "Gotta Have Civility? Gotta Have a Wawa." It read, in part:

> *Does it sometimes seem like the world's moving*
> *backward in the civility department?*
>
> *The war in Iraq, the war in Afghanistan and closer to*

home, the settling of disputes with handguns right here in the streets of Philadelphia.

With all that chaos in the world stressing your mind, here's a suggestion with a bright ray of hope: Go to your nearest Wawa store.

I can't help but wonder if anybody sees what I see every time I go through the doors of a Wawa store. No matter who it is, little old lady, leather-wearing biker, tattooed scary looking guy, belligerent teenager, everybody holds the door open for someone else.

And when a door is held for someone, it never fails, they always say thank you. Always ...

Who knows? Common courtesy, civility and world peace might be right around the corner at a Wawa store.

Of course, it's the Wawa associates who play the biggest role in creating delightful person-to-person experiences. Wawa is about friends and neighbors serving friends and neighbors. Here are some typical examples:

- In Longwood, Pennsylvania, a customer burst into our store frustrated one day because she couldn't figure out how to use the gas pump. (She was from New Jersey, where self-service gas pumps are legally barred.) A Wawa associate went outside and pumped the gas for her. While there, the customer told him she had just lost someone very, very close to her and started crying. She was obviously having a really bad day and just needed someone to share a few moments with. When her gas tank was full, she gave the associate a warm hug and left.

- Another time, a man had a heart attack at the Wawa store in Media, Pennsylvania. Kathleen Koury, the manager on duty, called 911 and performed CPR while waiting for an ambulance to arrive. Afterward, the store maintained contact with the man's family. Fortunately, he had a full recovery and, to show his appreciation, returned to the store a month later with his family and a big cake for the store's associates.

- A few years ago, shortly before Thanksgiving, an assistant manager in Kristen McDevitt's Media, Pennsylvania, store heard that one of her everyday customers, a wheelchair-bound man living far from family and friends, would be all alone for the holiday. Kristin made him a plate of Thanksgiving dinner. The gesture brought him to tears.

- One day while John Luidens was managing our store in Narbeth, Pennsylvania, a neighbor came in complaining about a nearby trash can that was overflowing and sending garbage into an intersection by the store. It wasn't a Wawa trash can, but one that was supposed to be maintained by the township. "We emptied it that day," John says, "and we also made sure that on a daily basis that trash can was checked to make sure it wasn't overflowing and trash wasn't spewing all over the intersection. Not only did the man who complained come in and thank us, but as the story circulated, a number of people who lived close by also came in and thanked us."

- We don't offer drive-through service at Wawa, but Tracy Pappa's store in Avondale, Pennsylvania, has a customer in his nineties who rates a little extra service. He visits that store every day, sometimes several times a day, and Tracy's associates go out of their way to help him gather his groceries and carry his purchases out to the car. Tracy now manages one of our new Florida stores and was part of the initial manager team charged with spreading Wawa's culture in the Sunshine State.

- Paul Halko's store in Newtown Square, Pennsylvania, is located on a busy thoroughfare, Route 252 (Providence Road). "A customer came in one time and told the associate working the cash register that his car had broken down on 252 with a flat tire," Paul says. "The associate asked me if he could go out and help him, for which I applauded him. It so happens we're right next door to a fire station, so while he helped change the flat, I arranged with them to divert traffic so that my associate wouldn't get hurt." The curious part of the story is that the man came to Wawa for help with his tire rather than the fire station, which was probably better equipped for such emergencies. But I guess that says something about the kind of reputation Wawa tends to get in the neighborhoods we serve.

We never told our people to do these things. There is nothing in any Wawa manual that directs associates to fix a flat tire, lend a shoulder to cry on, or take dinner to customers' houses. Wawa associates do these things on their own because they want to delight their customers.

Many years ago, I had stopped at a Wawa location in Upper Darby, Pennsylvania. A woman walked in who was clearly emotional. She grabbed me and said, "You work for the company? You must be an executive." (I had a tie and a jacket on.)

"Yes, ma'am," I said.

"I've got to tell you this," she said. "A couple of weeks ago, my mother passed away. It happened unexpectedly and I had only a day or two to make all the arrangements. I was preparing to bring the family together, ordering food. I was emotionally distraught until I came into Wawa. I was not a regular customer, but your employees could tell I was upset. When I walked into the store sobbing, they took me aside, offered me a cup of coffee and said, 'What can we do to help?' Now I'm a customer for life. Your people did something that no one else took the time to do even though I went to other places where I was a regular customer."

Jack, the Coffee Tastes Better When You Make It!

Jack Paul was in a local delicatessen in Philadelphia having brunch with Sarah, his wife of sixty-three years, when a young man approached their table. He was a customer at the Wawa convenience store where Jack worked three mornings a week. The young man greeted Jack and told him that he had dropped in to the Wawa that morning for a cup of coffee, and it didn't taste nearly as good as it did when Jack was there making it. Jack smiled, thanked the young man, and then turned to his wife and said with a laugh, "Sarah, nice man, but how could the coffee taste better when I make it? It's Wawa brand coffee, supplied in premeasured pouches; the water comes out of a filtered tap directly into the coffee machine. How could it possibly taste better when I make it?"

When Jack—who is my dad—told me this story later, I explained what the young man meant. "Dad, you make the coffee taste better." "I do?" "Sure you do. It's because you like people, you're nice to them, and you're interested in them. You share yourself with them,

make them laugh, and give them an upbeat start to the day. You do naturally what organizations strive to do to attain and maintain success—you create a positive experience for your customers."

Excellence! Jack Paul got it, and so did his customers!

On a freezing cold January day in 2009, Jack was laid to rest. When I got up to deliver my eulogy, I was awestruck by how many of the folks crowded into the funeral home I didn't know. I did not speak of Jack's being a devoted friend and family man or the fact that he was twice decorated for bravery as a World War II paratrooper. Instead, I spoke about how Jack taught us that we all could make someone's life a little brighter, and I shared with them the story of how he had made the coffee taste better.

. . . .

Excerpted by permission from Harry Paul, John Britt & Ed Jent. *Who Kidnapped Excellence?* Berrett-Koehler Publishers, Inc., 2014.

We didn't tell the associates to do it; they wanted to help a distraught woman because it was the right thing to do.

For many of our customers, coffee is the most important thing they need to start their day. I'm sure you know somebody like that; you may even be somebody like that.

One of the regulars at Jason Boyer's store in West Chester, Pennsylvania, is a woman who cares for a husband at home with long-term health issues. This woman—I'll call her Betty—looks forward to her time at Wawa as a much needed break, and Jason knows that she'll be in almost daily to buy a coffee-to-go box.

Sometimes our stock of food or supplies runs out before we can restock. And one day, the store's coffee host, Charlie Carbin, told Jason, "We're out of coffee-to-go boxes. And Betty needs her coffee! I'm going to lend her one of our backup coffee pots." Even for Wawa, this is a pretty wacky idea. But lacking another option for serving such a regular customer, Jason sent her home with a $200 coffee pot, which she promised to return the next day. Unfortunately, a snowstorm hit and Betty couldn't get back as planned. At least she had plenty of coffee while she waited!

Our Glen Mills general manager, Denise Haley, got a phone call at the store from one of her regular customers, Teresa. She is eighty-nine years old, and she always calls ahead to have the store gather items that she plans to purchase once she arrives. Denise always gives her a warm welcome when she enters the store. She even goes as far as to give her a hard time when she isn't using her cane. One day, however, Teresa called the store and asked for Denise. She had fallen in her house, which is located behind our store. Denise had finished work at 2:00 p.m., but she still happened to be there to take the call. She immediately ran over to the house to help Teresa. Teresa refused to let her call an ambulance. Denise went out of her way to drive her to the ER. After the ER visit, she even picked up her prescription medicine for her. She took hours out of her day to aid this sweet, elderly woman. Denise truly values people.

If stories like these make you think that Wawa people have a habit of going out of their way to provide extraordinary levels of service, you're right. We hear thousands of stories like these. It's all part of living the value of delighting our customers.

EMBRACE CHANGE

Wawa's two-hundred-year history is one of continuous change. Relentless innovation, reinvention, and "swimming upstream" are hallmarks of our success. But successful change means walking a fine line between preserving the underlying DNA of the business while changing strategies to make sure we're aligned with the marketplace.

When I started at Wanamaker's more than forty-five years ago, that legendary department store named after the man who invented the entire category seemed like the Rock of Gibraltar; I just assumed it would be there forever. I had friends who worked at other "Rocks" of the era: Gimbels, Lit Brothers, and Strawbridge & Clothier. None of those retailers exist today. They all lost their way and failed to change with the times. At Wawa, we remain solidly grounded thanks to our moral compass of shared private ownership and servant leadership even as we embrace change, learn from our failures, and take the business to the next level so the competition can't sprint past us.

The most important part about embracing change isn't so much the change itself. It's getting people to understand the reason for the change and the benefits it promises. If our associates and our customers don't understand the journey we're on, they'll travel elsewhere. So we spend a lot of time educating people and soliciting their feedback about prospective changes to our business. A lot of companies simply go into their ivory tower, dream of concepts, and initiate them. But if the organization isn't aligned, if it doesn't value and appreciate change, even the best idea will wither and die on the vine.

Change keeps an organization young. Of course, not everything we do will succeed. We're going to have failures. Facing up to those failures early on, making corrections, and being willing to let people fail leads to improvement. If we become too cautious an organization, there is no way that we will properly embrace change. Being nimble, agile, resilient, and willing to call an audible at the line of scrimmage will carry people along with us.

We didn't invent change. But we are good at mainstreaming new trends. Sometimes it might take us a year or two after the trend becomes visible and viable. Other times it may take us two decades, as in the case of specialty coffees. We could have made the decision to introduce those beverages ten years sooner, but we probably would not have done it right. We would have disappointed the customer, and that would have created a negative halo over our brand.

Sometimes we might embrace a little too much change all at once, at least in the eyes of some of our store managers.

"In 2012, we had to embrace change many times—new equipment, new products, and new promotional lines," according to store manager Don Toogood. "We got a new register system, a new fresh bread baking program, and we had new promotions going on at the same time. We had a new customer service rollout. Things were changing all the time!"

Don says it all worked out in the end, but only because he communicated the changes to his associates.

"I never wait until the last minute to tell my team," Don says. "And I do it with an upbeat attitude, embracing it myself, telling them that I care about their opinions. I ask them to please only talk positively about changes when talking with customers. We have to get our team on board. Once we did that, change flew."

Ivan Jackson, manager of our store in Logan Township, New Jersey, says, "Change is the biggest part of Wawa. The ability to change and adapt to what's going on around us, from gasoline to espressos to roll baking, is why we're always on par or sometimes ahead of the competition. We're willing to take a chance and sometimes make a mistake if it will make Wawa something special. We want to be the leader and the best in everything we do. And if we have to change to do it, we have no problem doing so."

Another huge change for Wawa was our foray into fuel. There has never been a fuel retailer that could keep its image of appetizing food. Can you think of one? Can you think of a gas station that has a restaurant-quality image? And we're judged by the company we keep. When customers drive down the highway and see gas, they don't expect to see it accompanied by great food. So we worried it might be seen as a disconnect. Not so. Wawa customers told us that we do food very well, so why not fuel, too?

The move into fuel service worked for Wawa because we managed the process correctly. When the time was right, we didn't hire people from Exxon, Sunoco, or Texaco. We selected Jim Bluebello, a fellow who had been in store operations, and made him project leader. He learned everything he could about the fuel business, with help and training from QuikTrip. (In return, we taught them everything we could about the food business.) Jim went on to become our vice president of fuel and supply. He put together a team of ambitious Wawa associates that created a gasoline retail model that pretty much remains the same almost twenty years and three hundred new fuel stores later.

It's a wonderful feeling, an amazing accomplishment to have seen our people teach themselves an entirely new business—create, open, and perfect the model; learn from experience, mistakes, and success; and finally gain the number one market share in our market. There were plenty of obstacles to overcome along the way. No one wanted us to succeed. The competition, and even some customers, didn't think there was a need for another major gas retailer in the marketplace.

Our competitors weren't willing to sell us product, so we had to create a supply portfolio that created independence for us and guaranteed a supply channel. The worst thing would have been to build gasoline stations and not have gas to sell. We initially bought product locally, from Mid-Atlantic regional distributors. Later, as the number of gas stores grew, we purchased product from the Colonial Pipeline, which originates at the Gulf of Mexico.

Around 2009, we began importing product from Great Britain and storing it in tanks owned by Magellan Midstream Partners, LP, at the Port of Wilmington, Delaware. That made us supply independent in that no competitor could pull the plug on us. There were hurricanes and other weather events that resulted in major shortages of fuel for our traditional competitors, but we hardly ever ran out of fuel.

During Hurricane Sandy in late 2012, many other retailers, including the major brands, simply switched off their lights, turned off their pumps, and went home. Wawa was one of the few gas retailers that remained open throughout the storm and could satisfy customers' needs.

Compared to food, fuel is volatile in more ways than one. The price is ever changing, as is supply and demand. In fact, the price of fuel can easily and dramatically increase, sometimes overnight. If something goes on in the Middle East, or if there is simply a hint of impending trouble, fuel skyrockets and shortages are created. A single oil refinery goes offline and there will be a fuel shortage. If a hurricane threatens in the Gulf of Mexico, there will be a fuel shortage. It's completely unlike anything we ever dealt with previously in the stores. It's completely unlike deli, coffee, or the general convenience business. There is no food product in our stores that's going to similarly rise in terms of price. We've learned to cope with these uncertainties and smooth the bumps in the road for our customers—all part of the change process we've mastered at Wawa.

Personal change can also be challenging—but ultimately rewarding. Dick Wood liked to move people around from one leadership role to another. He felt that a good manager should be able to manage a number of different functions, from real estate and strategic planning to human resources or marketing. Dick and I were always tolerant of the possibility that people might fall on their face, as long as they learned from the experience. Over time, they learned how to expand their skills in the process. It's another example of how we try to embrace change every day at Wawa.

DO THINGS RIGHT

If you've seen our stores, you may have wondered why coffee condiments are on an island separate from where the coffeepots are brewing. They're there to ensure that customers have more room to complete the preparation of their coffee, and that new customers have plenty of room to pour their coffee.

This didn't happen by accident. It happened by design. It is a design that was developed, tested, modified, and retested dozens of times by a team—a combination of marketing, operations, operations engineering, and store design departments. They measure, count, and observe the reactions of customers and adjust our designs accordingly.

There is an oft-repeated rhyme in our industry: Retail is detail. This is part of the Wawa ethos as well. We stock more than three thousand products in each of our stores, from hoagies to pretzels to iced tea, and everything we sell moves out the doors in high volume. We complete more than 500 million customer transactions a year. We are the customers' kitchen and we can't violate their trust. Customers must know that their meals are cooked to the correct temperature, they're of high quality, and they're safe.

Consistency leads to predictability, which in turn leads to enduring customer relationships. The proof is being able to do things right repetitively and seamlessly. Well-engineered processes free our associates to deliver great customer service. If they're constantly putting out fires because we don't have smart processes in place, then that takes away from the customer's experience.

However, being consistently excellent is easier said than done. It requires measurements and processes in place to guarantee that high quality. We engineer our stores with processes that aren't overly complicated so that 21,000 associates can orchestrate and follow them. Doing things right from a brand protection and a customer relations standpoint is vital to our survival. If there are issues or discrepancies, we want to know about it before our customers tell us—and eighteen of their friends and family—about it.

When we do fall short, customers are vocal and willing to share the positives and negatives with us—the latter usually more loudly and clearly. We learn from those negative experiences and are grateful for them. You have to be willing to accept the help of others in order to become better.

At the sametime, we make an extra effort to get it right the first time. It's never easy, but meeting that never-ending challenge is part of the fun of living the Wawa way.

DO THE RIGHT THING

If "doing things right" is about maintaining the consistent quality of our products, services, and processes, "doing the right thing" is about setting priorities. It stands for Wawa's commitment to practicing the highest ethical standards, contributing to the economic and social well-being of the communities we serve, and doing everything we can to enhance the quality of life enjoyed by our customers, our associates, and every other group of people whose lives we touch.

Doing the right thing sometimes carries a cost. It may require an investment with no immediate or obvious return; it may mean turning away an opportunity for quick gain that might damage our reputation in the long run. But we believe that, over time, doing the right thing is also smart business. We believe that retail customers want to identify with organizations that have high ethics, and we believe that the most talented store associates want to work for organizations that occupy the high moral ground. And over the past decades, doing the right thing has created a remarkable superhighway for Wawa, thanks to the positive relationships we've established and maintained with millions of people who've come to know and love us.

There are many specific components to doing the right thing, and every great company makes its own decisions about how to focus its energies. For Wawa, doing the right thing includes respecting and protecting the environment, supporting children's programs, fighting hunger, practicing open communication, and treating our suppliers and contractors fairly, as partners in a team effort. We try to practice these disciplines continually and without fanfare, and when we slip up we move quickly to acknowledge our mistake and rectify the damage.

A few years ago, I spoke to a group of fifty CEOs about the Wawa experience. I was scheduled to follow that with forty-five minutes of Q&A. But

Inspiring Others to Be Fit to Fly

In 2010, the Wawa family embarked on our Fit to Fly wellness journey. From biometric screenings to discounts on healthy products in-store, our associates now have access to many resources to help them in their wellness journey. But nothing is more powerful than the encouragement and inspiration a friend or fellow associate can provide to keep us on track. It's something we refer to in our Fit to Fly Five: "Inspire Others."

James Broglin, from store 360 in Sewell, New Jersey, wrote a letter about how a fellow associate named Jim encouraged him on his journey by going to the gym with him and sharing fitness routines. Jim was so committed to helping James succeed that he continued to do so even after moving to a store more than forty-five minutes away. Here's an excerpt from James's letter:

In June of 2012, when I went to a regular doctor's appointment, they found a lump on my leg and thought it might be cancer. Thankfully, it wasn't. But it taught me I had to change my ways and get healthy for my family and more importantly for myself. So I started another diet. This wasn't my first attempt. I have always been overweight. I would lose some weight and then gain it all back.

In October 2012, I met Jim as he became our new inventory merchandise manager. I heard that he liked to go to the gym, so one day I asked him if he would be willing to help me by showing me how to do some exercises. Thankfully, he said yes, and the rest is history.

We started to work out one to two days a week in November of 2012. In December, Jim was transferred to the Elk Township Wawa store 435. I was devastated. I thought Jim might not want to work out any more. But he still wanted to help me. This meant the world to me! When I started all these workouts, they were not easy for me, but Jim just pushed me to do my best, and, boy, was he patient! As of now, I have lost 100 pounds. I went from a size 60 to a size 44 in pants . . .

I would like to recognize Jim for his values. Jim has never asked for anything in return. He just wanted to help me. He wouldn't even take any gas money! Jim has taught me so much. Not just all the exercises, but also he has taught me how to have an incredible heart.

instead of questions, all I heard were testimonials. People felt compelled to stand up and talk about what Wawa meant to them.

The CEO of a software company who came over from India said he had been very successful in Philadelphia. He brought his parents, both in their early seventies, to join him here. He said, "You saved my father's life. He was lost. Foreign country, didn't speak the language, knew no one. Wawa gave him a job; your company made him a coffee host. Now he is a celebrity in his new community! Everyone knows him by name. He knows everyone else by name. You sustained his life."

The president of a social services company said, "You don't know what your company means to me. I have a special-needs son who is autistic. He can work your touchscreen computer and order his own lunch at Wawa, which makes him feel independent. But more importantly, your people make him feel like he's important, very important."

In the end, it's the customers who judge our quality. If we make them happy, and do so every single time they visit one of our stores, then we're doing our job the way we need to.

Another example of our commitment to doing the right thing is our effort to support families by supplying our heavy cream to kids suffering from epilepsy-related disorders.

"My son has a disorder, acquired aphasia, that started when he was about six years old," explains Lydia Melnyk. "After trying medication as a solution, the doctor put him on the ketogenic diet."

According to the Epilepsy Foundation, the ketogenic diet "forces the child's body to burn fat around the clock by keeping carbohydrates (sugars) low and making fat products the primary food the child is getting. In fact, the diet gets most (80 percent) of its calories from fat. The rest come from carbohydrates (sugars) and protein (meat). Each meal has about four times as much fat as protein or carbohydrate."

In the best-case scenario, the diet stops the crippling seizures that affect so many children. That was the case with Lydia's son, who, through a program coordinated by Children's Hospital Philadelphia, received quarts of Wawa extra-heavy whipping cream free of charge. It was integral to her son's diet—and the diets of many children just like him. Lydia says:

> Around here, the Wawa Dairy was one of the few places you could actually get this extra-heavy cream. It has to have an extra-high fat content, and for three years they sent it to my house twice every week by FedEx on dry ice. The seizures cost him the ability to understand or express language. Imagine a six-year-old who can't talk or quite understand what you're saying. And within three weeks of going on the ketogenic diet, he was seizure-free. He's now twenty. So I love Wawa in so many different ways. Besides loving Wawa's food, I just love their philosophy.

Stories like Lydia's reinforce the fact that Wawa's family of customers, associates, and vendor partners are our most treasured resource. Maybe the best way we show our caring for this extended Wawa family is by making their safety our number one priority.

Every business experiences an accident occasionally. To improve our safety performance, we hired DuPont Safety Resources Business in 2000 to provide customized safety consulting and training at Wawa. Safety services were provided to the entire Wawa organization, the company headquarters at Red Roof, and the Wawa dairy warehouse and distribution center. The result has been a 76 percent reduction in associate incident rate and a decrease in the customer incident rate by half.

Another recent example of our commitment to doing the right thing is the hiring of our first-ever wellness manager, Ralph Lardieri.

The health and well-being of our associates is an issue we care a lot about at Wawa. We want our associates to be well for at least one simple reason: We've got this great ESOP that should be able to fund a happy and comfortable retirement, and we want our associates to live long enough to enjoy it! These are our friends and we want them to be healthy.

At the same time, wellness has become a business issue for many companies in the twenty-first century thanks to rising health insurance premiums. If we can help our associates become healthier, it will save us all a lot of money in the long run—a secondary reason, but an important one, that explains why supporting wellness is the right thing to do.

That's where Ralph Lardieri comes in. Ralph is known in some corners of corporate headquarters as "that guy who caused all the congestion on the stairs" because he strongly encourages everyone to skip the elevators and walk.

"That's true," Ralph says with a laugh. "That's a good, easy thing to do. We want people to move more. We call it the Fit to Fly Five—Eat Right, Move More, Quit Tobacco, Inspire Others, Have Fun—and part of it is to move more. Easy thing to do, especially if you work in an office building."

"I did my research on Wawa—what the company and its values were all about," Ralph says. "I told the people who interviewed me, 'Hey, if Wawa is really true to its values, wellness will be a big hit here.'"

His first week on the job, I ran into Ralph in a hallway. I told him that before starting anything, I wanted him to get to know our people, particularly in the stores, and develop ways we could help them as much as the people behind desks at Red Roof.

I told Ralph, "Listen, we're coming off ten years of changing the way we do business at the store level in terms of safety. We're a hundred miles into this three-thousand-mile wellness journey. It's going to take some time."

Ralph started doing on-site biometric screenings at the stores. We also offer a wellness discount at the store level. Associates get a discount on a lot of our food, but they can get a greater discount on salads, on sandwiches under 300 calories, and on fruits and vegetables. They can get a banana and a yogurt for a buck at our stores. That's a great price for a healthy meal. In the same way that safety is now an important part of the way we do business, I think wellness will get there as well.

Store general manager Debbie June is an enthusiastic proponent of the Wawa Wellness Program.

"As you get older, if you don't take care of yourself, nobody else is going to do it for you," she says. "I talk about it with my people: 'Wawa truly cares about us and all the programs that they put forth like the wellness program exist for our well-being, for our health. They want to help us keep healthy and fit, so we can help grow the business. There are not many companies that will pre-screen associates and at the same time give us recognition for doing it.'"

Is the well-being of our associates really something the leaders at Wawa should be concerned about? We think so—and we are also concerned about the safety of our workforce, the environmental health of our communities, and the economic vibrancy of the neighborhoods where our stores are located. When we look back on our careers, we want to be able to say that the world is a little better place because of the way we conducted ourselves at Wawa. It's all part of doing the right thing.

HAVE A PASSION FOR WINNING

At Wawa, we thrive on competition. It unleashes creativity and extraordinary performance. We mix hard work and fun. We know there is not one single finish line that will mark our ultimate success, but we have the passion and determination to achieve any goal. That is winning, and it reinforces commitment and inspires confidence, self-esteem, and pride.

We are never satisfied. Instead, we constantly strive to redefine what Wawa and convenience retailing are all about. That's a very high standard to which we hold ourselves every day. We know what we think we can achieve, we create plans to achieve it, we dream big, and we measure ourselves against those dreams. It's not about beating any one competitor; it's about setting the bar higher and higher, continually doing better today than we did yesterday.

Scott Hambridge is an area manager for Wawa who has been with the company in various positions for more than twenty-five years. He demonstrated his passion for winning in the way he handled a very tough customer at our closest store to Philadelphia International Airport.

It was 3:30 in the morning when the customer walked in with his wife, hungry for a couple of our signature breakfast sandwiches. Scott recounts what happened:

> *The customer wanted Sizzlis®, and we don't usually start them until 4:30 a.m. But I said, "What kind do you want? I'll make them for you right now." He told me, so I went over and immediately put them in.*
>
> *The breakfast sandwiches only take four minutes from start to finish—assembling, cooking. But the man was impatient. He kept complaining to the cashier: "This is ridiculous. Why do I have to wait?"*
>
> *He was pacing back and forth. It turned out he was on his way to the airport to fly to Hawaii. He obviously needed the stress relief of an island vacation.*

I felt bad for the guy's wife, because she was clearly embarrassed by the way that he was acting. She ended up going to the car to wait after her threshold had been reached. The guy was very rude both to me and the cashier.

I saw him again a couple of weeks later and he was a lot more relaxed.

I said, "How was your trip to Hawaii? What island did you go to?" I went out of my way to engage him, and he was a lot nicer this time. I don't know if he remembered me or the way he treated me, but to me that didn't matter. Obviously, despite his frustration that previous day, he still viewed us as somewhere where he wanted to go because he was back.

That was a Wawa victory for Scott, a triumph just as tangible as a sports trophy or an Academy Award. It was the kind of small victory that happens every day at Wawa.

Of course, we're also constantly looking for ways to increase our competitive advantage. We do a lot of market research in which we ask several key questions: "Where would you rather shop?" "How frequently do you shop Wawa compared to other retailers you could go to?" "How likely are you to return?" and "Would you recommend Wawa to a friend?"

The answers to those questions are what it's about. We want customers to shop us more frequently than other retailers, to admire us at a higher level, and to recommend us more enthusiastically to other customers.

It may sound unbelievable, but we get letters all the time from folks who've moved away from the Philadelphia area telling us that the thing that they miss the most is that Wawa experience. Ken Markizon of Wilmington, Delaware, wrote:

About eighteen months ago, I sent you a letter detailing how much I loved Wawa. I had told you how much my wife and I appreciate the convenience and the consistency. Now I need to take a moment to bring to your attention something that happened last week.

My father stopped into your store at 400 Wilson Road in Wilmington. He got lightheaded and fell. Your first shift

Greg Soto and the Meaning of Winning

Even before April 16, 1964, when Grahame Wood placed the Wawa name on the first store in Folsom, Pennsylvania, the company had earned a reputation for being value driven. However, it was not until the 1990s that approximately thirty Wawa associates came together with the assignment to identify and codify our six core values. Thirty people were selected from a cross-section of the company, including operations, the dairy, the call center, finance, human resources, and marketing, and represented all levels in the organization except for the vice presidents and CEO.

They were asked to search deep down into the soul of the company to find the few right words to say who we at Wawa are and what we want to be known for, now and forever.

By early afternoon, the team had agreed on five of the six values. But the sixth value, a passion for winning, was still under discussion.

"Yes," said one of the participants, "winning is a guiding value, but we need to understand better what those words mean at Wawa. Are the words too confrontational? Does it focus too much on beating the competition or on making money? At Wawa, a passion for winning has to be about something bigger than just those things.

At that point, manager Greg Soto stood up to offer the following story: *When I was a brand new store manager in a brand new store, our*

staff there went above and beyond in helping out my dad.
Becky called 911 and then got my mom's phone number
and called her as well to let her know what was going on.
Dad went to the hospital and was found to be anemic and
dehydrated. You'd have to know my father to appreciate
this, but his main concern throughout the episode was the
safety of his two Wawa coffee mugs that he brought into the

associates agreed to sponsor a Little League baseball team. We took a photo of that team of kids and we hung it prominently on the wall. We invited parents, players, and the community to stop by the store and see it.

That was over a dozen years ago, and now that wall has over a dozen photos of different teams. Those kids grew up, they became parents themselves, and now they come by with their kids. For me and my team, that is winning.

The reaction of the committee was unanimous. All thirty of them agreed that our sixth value would be a passion for winning as defined by Greg Soto.

In December 2012, that store turned twenty-five years old, and we held a celebration on-site. Greg was there, just as he had been since the store first opened. It was jam-packed with customers, community leaders, and Wawa people, all of whom had come to love and admire Greg and his wife, Colleen, for the things they had achieved for the store and the community. The local US congressman even traveled to the store to present Greg and Colleen with an American flag and a plaque honoring Greg's charitable service and civic work.

As for Greg's wall display, it was covered with Little League teams, one for every year that Wawa played a leading role in the community. Not a bad portrait of what a passion for winning means at Wawa.

store. Becky rescued the mugs off of the floor, secured them in the back, and kept them in safekeeping until my dad had a chance to get them back.

Of course, the coffee mugs serve as a light side note to the story. But, please know that you have good people that care about doing the right thing for others. Pass along my thanks to Becky and her team. Their efforts and clear-headedness meant a lot to me, my mom & dad, and our family. I hope all is well for you.

P.S.: Good luck in Florida, I think you guys will kill it down there.

Another customer, Denise Hadden, wrote:

I grew up in Delaware where Wawa was a staple. Coffee, wraps, subs, stuffed pretzels, salads ... oh, it was all a part of my daily routine. Then, nine years ago, I married Benjamin, a military man, and we moved to Italy for three years. Every single trip home included a stop at the first Wawa we came across. Nothing said home like that fresh cup of Wawa coffee. Pure Heaven! It didn't matter that we lived in Italy—the land of coffee—nothing could replace our Wawa coffee. Each trip home, we filled up as much as we could with all of our Wawa goodies.

Now, we live in Annapolis, Maryland. I have to say, the house we picked was a bit more loved because it has a Wawa right around the corner. To me, it kind of feels like the show Cheers—it's the place where everybody knows my name.

Our Six Core Values

At Wawa, our passion for winning isn't necessarily about boosting our profit margins or raising our stock price (important as those things may be). It's about creating many more Ken Markizons and Denise Haddens—devoted fans and friends who've made Wawa an essential part of their daily lives.

Wawa believes in convenience and value and has always had a surcharge-free ATM policy in every one of its stores.

CHAPTER 8

Surviving the Dark Days

> The good-to-great companies faced just as much adversity as the comparison companies, but responded to that adversity differently. They hit the realities of their situation head-on. As a result, they emerged from adversity even stronger.
>
> —**Jim Collins**, *Good to Great*

When I joined Wawa in 1987, the company was going through significant challenges. Dick Wood called this period Wawa's Dark Days, and they were extremely painful.

We were having trouble recruiting and retaining associates at the store level. Turnover was extremely high. Our brand reputation as an employer was questionable. Competition from supermarkets continued to erode the provisioning business that had been the foundation of Wawa sales.

The marketplace was changing. In the past, customers had been willing to pay a premium for convenience. Now more and more places were becoming convenient. Supermarkets were proliferating and becoming as ubiquitous as convenience stores, expanding their hours and doing away with quaint but expensive policies that had them closed on Sundays. Simultaneously, McDonald's and other quick-service restaurants were opening everywhere.

We held our collective breath because the number of people coming through our doors was declining, profits were falling, and the Wawa stock price dropped for the first time. It was scary.

Wawa was still the dominant retailer of made-to-order hoagies and coffee in our home region, but they weren't enough. Attempts to develop hot food products had failed. Fifty stores experimented with grills, some of which generated strong customer demand, but none were profitable enough to sustain growth or suggest roll out to the rest of the chain. In some stores, enterprising managers brought in hot plates from home and heated up canned soup for their customers. We eventually put an end to this well-intended idea because of product safety concerns—food-borne illness is always our most important concern. All we had to show for our efforts in the hot food arena were hot dogs.

It became apparent that the company would have to reinvent itself—again. Wawa needed to do three things: Build its own food brand; develop superior skills, partners, and processes; and offer customers both fast service and choices of real food that tasted more like home.

In retrospect, it all sounds simple enough, but at the time the path was far from clear. Despite the incredible sales and unit growth Wawa had achieved before and would again in the future, our successful escape from the Dark Days didn't come without a strong dose of trauma.

Going back into my files as I researched this book, I discovered that the Dark Days were darker than I'd even remembered. As I reviewed old shareholder reports and memos, it became more and more apparent that our business back then was really in free fall. In 1989, for example, customer traffic decreased 2.3 percent per store week according to our in-house tracking.[5] In 1990, customer traffic decreased another 3.1 percent. Then, in the first part of 1991, customer traffic was down 5 percent more.

In the midst of this, I joined Wawa as the vice president of human resources. My previous employer had been The Limited clothing chain, where I spent time both on the retail side at the Columbus, Ohio, headquarters and then in Boston on the manufacturing side.

The Limited was a personal transformation for me in terms of forgetting everything I'd learned previously. It was the on-the-job equivalent of going to Harvard Business School. The Limited always stretched its people, and we did things we didn't previously think we were capable of doing.

Soon after I started at Wawa, Dick Wood asked me about my experiences at The Limited. At The Limited you were trained to think big, set huge goals, and go after them. Reflecting on this philosophy, I said to Dick, "Here at Wawa, the sum total of the parts don't add up to anything. We need to simplify. We need to edit down, and we need to do a few new things and do them bigger and better."

Until that point, our people were testing all kinds of unrelated product concepts. We said, "Let's kill 90 percent of them."

We came up with this concept called Item Killer and printed T-shirts for our associates. We had everyone come in with all their ideas, and we worked hard to get down to a few big ideas that could make a real difference in our struggling business. Getting people to give up their "passion projects" and narrow down what they were doing was a big challenge.

It wasn't too long after that that Dick said to me, "Howard, I want you to go into marketing."

---

5 "Per store week" is an industry term used by management to describe key business measurements on an average weekly basis based on all stores in aggregate.

I knew nothing about marketing, except to the extent that at The Limited everybody was trained to think like a marketing executive. But Dick insisted: "You're in HR, and you're building the people brand there. You can now rebuild the marketing brand. We need to think differently."

I called a management meeting and showed up with a giant crayon—it would become my personal trademark among our associates—and an oversized THINK BIG coffee cup.

At the time, we already had Don Price, who became known as our "Minister of the Magic," on our leadership team, but we lacked an organizational structure of a traditional marketing department. We had decentralized field-marketing people in each of eight different regions in five states who did field marketing and product development on a part-time basis. We also had centralized procurement and advertising departments. We created a centralized marketing organization and a category management structure modeled on what worked so well at The Limited.

We knew, in terms of organizational concepts and design, what made sense for the business and that we had to get our hands around our brand proposition, that we had to let the consumer know what we stood for.

We needed to be much more aggressive and establish unique programs, products, and concepts that would drive the business forward. We couldn't just serve or sell products of others and be Ye Olde General Store. We had to be something else.

Meanwhile, the financial struggles continued. We told our associates, "Flat sales don't mean flat earnings. Flat sales mean declining earnings." We had bloodletting meetings every Saturday focused mainly on cost-cutting measures. The most creative suggestion anyone offered might be "Maybe, we can sell off another Xerox machine to save money."

This had to change. We finally attacked the problem from the opposite direction. "We've got to invest. We've got to always invest in our people. They have the answers."

We took several major steps to halt our losses. Our famous made-to-order sandwiches were officially branded "Wawa Hoagies," with three sizes for the first time, to give customers the choices they asked for: "Classic®," "Shorti®," and "Junior®." To attract traffic, we set lower prices on beverages, including twelve-packs of soda, and we lowered our prices on tobacco.

That last move was a tactic that Dick Wood learned from Sheetz, another Pennsylvania convenience store chain. Dick proposed dropping our tobacco prices as low as the law allowed. Dropping those prices would clearly have a negative short-term impact on profitability. We'd previously earned $0.55 per pack on cigarettes, but we took it down to a margin of just $0.11 a pack. We had to sell five times as many cigarettes to match the same margin. That's a lot of tobacco. But our biggest concern was getting customers in the door. Without that steady stream of visitors, the viability of the company would be questionable. Lower tobacco prices could provide us with the traffic we desperately needed.

There was an obvious moral dilemma there. Tobacco sales, admittedly, were controversial internally and externally. Years earlier, we'd stopped selling *Playboy*, *Penthouse*, and other adult-content magazines as not fitting our values. And we didn't sell rolling papers, used mostly for marijuana, as a lot of convenience store retailers profitably did.

But at that time, a quarter of Americans were smokers. We had to reconcile, within the organization, our value system against our brand offer and our proposition to the consumer. There were plenty of people within the company who didn't feel comfortable with the new strategy, including members of the Wood family. We wrestled with that dilemma because, from a health standpoint, we didn't even want our own associates or family members to smoke.

It was probably one of the biggest values-conflicted business decisions we ever made. But in retail, the choice was clear: Be competitive on pricing or face the prospect of a quarter of customers going elsewhere for their cigarettes . . . and their milk and sandwiches. Other stores, including drugstores, which seemed particularly counterintuitive to good health practices, were taking market share from us. If "healthy" businesses like drugstores were increasing their market share in tobacco, how could we not embrace the opportunity?

We decided to give the new strategy a test in our stores located in Pennsylvania's Lehigh Valley. We went big and bold in Allentown, buying billboards everywhere: LOWEST CIGARETTE PRICES ALLOWED BY LAW. We took out full-page newspaper ads with the same message. The test paid immediate dividends as customer count grew. Not only did we sell enough cigarettes to recoup our lost gross profit but those customers were coming in and buying our food service products.

We reviewed the results and Dick quickly decided to roll the strategy out to the balance of the company's stores. It was amazing what a jolt the competitive pricing strategy gave our business. Because the perception of value was so strong, customers quickly formed new shopping habits around their neighborhood Wawa. Within one year, from the first quarter of 1991 to the first quarter of 1992, traffic went up 14.7 percent.

Promoting cheap cigarettes was controversial and generated articles and letters from antismoking groups. But cigarette smokers supported our coffee and hoagie sales in a big way. For that large segment of our customers, we were doing the right thing. We used our traffic-building cigarette strategy as a way of educating consumers as to how we were building Wawa for the future. Tobacco was a major bridge strategy for us.

That experience transformed us as an organization. It taught us that we could control our destiny, it taught us to think big, and it taught us that we could execute superbly. The campaign—with billboards, full-page newspaper ads, and in-store banners—was unlike anything previously attempted in our company's history. The tobacco campaign was the talk of Philadelphia and the convenience store industry because we made it bigger than life. It changed the way customers perceived the value we presented in everything going forward, from coffee and hoagies to no-ATM surcharges and gasoline.

Most important, it helped reassure those customers who wanted to shop Wawa for all of our other products that our pricing was fair. The campaign gave us permission, strength, and the conviction to do everything big. Before, we were like that neighborhood mom-and-pop deli, that small urban superette, or that general country store. We'd done a lot of things, but before this, we hadn't done anything big.

Within a relatively short period of time, we became the region's preferred retailer for cigarettes and we dramatically increased market share in this category. It was a major turning point in our history—the first shot fired in the revolution that defined our brand.

Today, the controversy over tobacco sales has subsided. Every retailer in our business sells tobacco. Drugstores continue to do it. Dollar stores do it. Mass merchants such as Walmart continue to do it, although Target does not. The good news is that Wawa is much less reliant on tobacco than we were twenty years ago because we now sell gasoline, offer surcharge-free ATM transactions, and food service as drivers. And as we open new stores, tobacco, in terms of its footprint and visual presentation, is less and less visible.

In the years since our tobacco campaign, anti-smoking forces in society have gained strength. Promoting and advertising cigarettes in the way we used to do it is now prohibited. We make the commitment to only sell cigarettes to those adults whom the law said were entitled to make the decision to smoke. We are strict about not selling to minors, and we conduct audits and develop systems to reinforce that determination.

In the final analysis, we weathered the storm. We took our hits, but we handled the public relations aspects, and today, as a result, we're a far stronger company. In hindsight, it was the right thing to do for all stakeholders, including the community, our vendor partners, our associates, and our customers.

By implementing value pricing for cigarettes, we retook control of our destiny. It was the start of a major redefinition of who we were.

And we knew it wasn't just our tobacco prices that were out of whack. We were charging too much for several other convenience store staples.

There are three basic reasons why we choose anything in life: function, emotion, and price. Take coffee, for example. The function of coffee is reflected in questions such as "Does it taste good?" and "Is it hot?" The emotion of coffee may be involved in factors like the way Rachel behind the counter at Wawa always says hello and makes me feel special. As for price, this is measured by the simple question "Is it worth it?"

Of those three drivers, we found that it was number three—"Is it worth it?"—on which we were out of whack. The fast feeders—places like McDonald's—had a price war going on that was affecting us. They all offered $0.99 meals.

So we lowered our prices dramatically. But cutting our prices meant we had to sell a whole lot more product just to break even. We did that slowly but surely by adding new products that customers couldn't find in other stores and food services that competed well with the fast feeders.

Today, we have the eighth-largest market share for coffee sales in the country and are dominant in the Philadelphia marketplace. We went big and bold on coffee—$0.59 a cup—to bring customers into the store.

We built huge displays of soda at just $2.99 per twelve-pack so that customers knew exactly what we stood for when they walked in. Every store had a mountainous display of Pepsi and Coke products with killer prices that made clear our value proposition.

Going big let the consumer know exactly what Wawa stood for. Eventually, the clouds parted and light began to shine through. The combination of these reconsidered, repriced, and rebranded product offerings began the long journey away from the Dark Days. They gave Wawa the stability necessary to invest in the competencies that helped us become a leader in on-the-go food service.

· · · · ·

In reinvigorating our business, it would be wrong to say we knew exactly what to do. In one particular case, in fact, we learned a valuable lesson by doing the exact wrong thing.

In the mid-1990s, Wawa's leadership team knew that, beyond hoagies, coffee, and soda, we lacked the kind of brand credibility enjoyed by such world-famous companies like McDonald's. We had yet to build the necessary competencies and infrastructure. We concluded that we needed the brands of others to rise above the competition and elevate Wawa to truly iconic stature.

At that time, Pizza Hut and Taco Bell were owned by PepsiCo Food Services, which was trying to think big in its own way by seeking out as many points of distribution as it could. We were, admittedly, seduced by the concept of attaching their brand identities to ours as a fast way of getting into the quick-service restaurant business.

Dick Wood and I went to Texas and benchmarked a convenience food store chain called Stop N Go that did co-branding. We met with their CEO, Pete Van Horn, and came away from that meeting convinced that it was something we should do. We tested Pizza Hut in around 20 stores, and Taco Bell in 125 stores. Our vendor partners were thrilled because we opened the door to hundreds of locations to sell tacos and pizza. They worked closely with us.

We simultaneously explored adding Dunkin' Donuts products using the logic that if we were in the coffee business, that opened the door wide to being in the bakery business as well. We put Dunkin' Donuts in the vast majority of our stores, again taking the co-branding shortcut.

But when we told our associates, "You're going to be making pizzas and tacos," they were anything but excited. They wanted to make Wawa products, not somebody else's branded meals. They could not get their hearts into the food service products of others.

Focus groups that we convened with customers told us we had made a terrible mistake. "That's a crazy idea," they told us in no uncertain terms. "How can you put a Pizza Hut or a Taco Bell in your store? If we want pizza, we'll go somewhere that specializes in pizza."

To the Mid-Atlantic consumer, Wawa was mainstream Americana, motherhood, and apple pie. Ethnic foods—Mexican and Italian—caused a disconnect in terms of the consumer experience and Wawa. Pizza Hut and Taco Bell didn't work at all for us, except in a small handful of our stores. Co-branding also failed because it took too much time, clogged up our then limited parking, produced slim margins, and the draw was not unique or compelling to our customers. As a result, it wasn't profitable enough to sustain the increased labor costs it brought us. Our timing was also off in entering the fast-food business. Prices were being squeezed and we got caught in the crossfire of value-pricing wars.

On the whole, co-branding failed miserably. Out of 150 stores where we had a co-brand, it worked well in 10.

The Dunkin' Donuts trial was more successful and might have made sense to continue under different circumstances. Their donuts sold well. But Dunkin' is a franchise system and we had to deal with dozens of independent operators who did not individually share our commitment to serve customers, making it a complicated partnership.

Dunkin' Donuts also created a beverage conflict for us. Dunkin' wanted us to sell their coffee, but we resisted because we were building our own coffee brand.

In moving away from Dunkin' Donuts, we partnered with a Frenchman named Alfred Neuhauser. He was making bagels for American hotels and cruise lines, although 95 percent of his business was back home in France. His US bakery, located not far from us in New Jersey, had the capability of doing fresh-baked products, so we hammered out an agreement making his company the exclusive bakery for Wawa. After a year or two, he sold the business to one of our existing partners, J&J Snack Foods, and to this day they're still running it for us.

I might as well admit this, too: The Texas convenience food store against which we had benchmarked the co-branding was acquired soon afterward. But their failure with co-branding, and ours, doesn't mean co-branding is always a bad idea. Travel around the country and you will see Dunkin' Donuts, Subway, Godfather's Pizza, and Dairy Queen in convenience stores and gas stations. For those who don't have the infrastructure or aren't willing to make a long-term commitment to building their own brand, it is a way of getting into the food service business. Hess, for example, does a lot of co-branding with Blimpie, Dunkin' Donuts, and others. It makes sense for them because Hess is an oil company and it doesn't have the food service infrastructure that we do.

For Wawa, however, co-branding was just a detour that failed. We threw in the towel and discovered a new direction.

Lesson learned: Always listen to your customer. Our customers may have had a deep respect for the products sold by Taco Bell and Pizza Hut, but not in our stores.

Instead, our customers told us, "You've *already* got a great brand." We undoubtedly undervalued our brand. It became a lightbulb-over-the-head moment: "Oh, the Wawa brand has value!" There was a halo that we'd established through our dairy for more than a hundred years. The Wawa name meant quality assurance and freshness to the consumer. We needed to nurture and manifest that brand image in everything we did.

The co-branding mistake made us much better. Ever since then, we've done a better job of responding to downward trends in the business. These failures put us on a whole new path of establishing a Wawa food service brand.

．　．　．　．　．

Twenty years after Wawa emerged from its darkest of Dark Days, we still talk about what happened in the early 1990s, because many of our associates today didn't work for us then. What we learned from the bad times needs to be remembered, shared, and rehashed at appropriate times.

We'll have dark days again. We all know it. Hopefully, they will be few and far between, but every business goes through business cycles, periods where we have significant growth and then growth slows and we have to regroup, rethink, renew, reenergize, refresh, and move on.

When you work your way through difficult times as an organization, it builds team spirit and confidence. Out of failure comes valuable lessons that need to be shared with the organization. Failure helps us fight complacency. And recognizing that we had difficulty in the past creates humility. We know we will have difficulty in the future, and we prepare ourselves for it.

In that sense, it's okay to be paranoid. In fact, Dick Wood always referred to himself as "the chief of paranoia." "If you don't worry," he says, "and if you don't think it can't happen to you, believe me, it will happen to you."

. . . . .

In addition to complacency, two of the greatest threats in business are arrogance and hubris. Trees don't grow to the sky. No business continues to grow and compound sales every single year at a high single-digit or double-digit rate. It simply doesn't happen. Sooner or later, reality catches up to you. It's caught up to the greatest companies in this nation.

We probably draw more on the difficult years than we do on the successes. We can't bury the failures because there are valuable lessons from the difficult times and we want to share them with our people. There are personal disappointments as well as business disappointments. They are huge learning opportunities.

The Dark Days were, in many ways, good days in that they were transformational. One of the things Wawa learned through its Dark Days was that we had to stay true to ourselves. There are so many organizations that, when external factors threaten, abruptly change strategies and do things that may be out of character, taking actions that customers quite honestly don't understand.

Customers had a perception of who we were and what we stood for. If we went too far outside those boundaries, thinking we could save the business or turn the business around, customers didn't feel good about it and didn't grant us permission to make the change. We had to stay true to ourselves and our brand.

During our Dark Days, Wawa customers felt their own pangs of economic anxiety. We learned that we can't publicly blame the economy in such times. So many companies point a finger at the economy for their downward spiraling sales and profits, but even in a bad economy, there are always windows of opportunity and silver linings. If we control our destiny in retail, we can seize opportunity by going after market share.

It's important at these times to keep things simple because the more complex things become, the more confusing they are in the customer's mind.

A particular characteristic that customers dislike is inconsistency. When customers don't feel good about where the economy is headed and they're worried day to day about their own positions, more than anything else they want the retailers they've trusted over the years to stay true to who they are. They need some things in their lives to remain constant; they want a friend they can trust.

This is what we learned: That our associates—the people on the front lines, interacting daily with customers—need to believe in what we do as a business. For that reason, it is as important to market internally as it is to market externally to customers because if our associates don't feel good, if they sense management's anxiety when times get rough, then customers are bound to feel it through our people.

Our associates are our best message communicators and marketing representatives, particularly when times get tough. When they know the direction of our company, what we are doing to grow sales and service their customers at the store level, it takes away their anxiety and it maintains the Wawa atmosphere and customer relationship prevalent in good times. We rely on our associates to be our best brand ambassadors at all times.

For this reason, we've always tried, even during the most difficult times, to continue investing in our associates through competitive wages, training, and ownership. There are companies that take advantage of hard times to freeze wages and benefits or cut retirement programs. At Wawa, that would fly in the face of our values. But more important, if we're going to work our way out of a difficult position, we need associates who will pull us out of the doldrums, who will stay positive until we all see light at the end of the tunnel. If they aren't pulling us toward the light, there is no way we're going to get where we need to go next.

When the US economy tanked in 2008, scores of companies cut wages and retirement benefits. We did none of that because, having gone through the Dark Days, we knew what to do, when to do it, how to react, and were still in control of our destiny. We actually strengthened our value proposition in 2008 and came out with a much better financial balance sheet.

We've sharpened our pencils every time we've gone through rough times by giving the customers more value in terms of price points. Value is also found in speed of service and quality in the heartfelt smile from an associate.

Business needs to be win-win for all stakeholders. During down economies, we've got to find a win for our customers, our associates, and our vendors. In 2008, we were all facing a painful recession, so we maintained our value proposition and stepped up promotional activity to make everyone feel better. Their resulting continued support, in turn, strengthened our financial balance sheet.

Embedded in our values is that our people pull together. When things go well, it's a team win. When things don't go well, the team draws closer and we work our way out of it together.

The Wawa culture and corporate DNA is such that we don't let people sink, we don't let people drown, and we don't let people fail. We provide a support structure that lifts them and the organization. That's what great organizations do.

We've always shied away from pointing the finger of blame at any one individual in most missteps. If we want to encourage risk taking and encourage people to step outside the known box and try new things, when things don't go right we don't want to penalize those people. We want to use them as an example. If anything, we want the organization to rally behind people when mistakes are made.

We remember the Dark Days with fondness—now that they're well behind us.

Wawa associates win the hearts of customers, not only through great in-store experiences, but through relationships and an unwavering commitment to supporting the communities they serve.

CHAPTER 9

Winning Share of Heart

Lovemarks reach your heart as well as your mind, creating an intimate, emotional connection that you just can't live without. Ever. Take a brand away and people will find a replacement. Take a Lovemark away and people will protest its absence. Lovemarks are a relationship, not a mere transaction. You don't just buy Lovemarks, you embrace them passionately. That's why you never want to let go. Put simply, Lovemarks inspire: Loyalty Beyond Reason.

—**Kevin Roberts,** *Lovemarks: The Future Beyond Brands*

Don Price arrived a little early for his job interview to become our first marketing director in 1979.

The location of the appointment was a Wawa store close to a factory, and when the factory let out at lunch, the store was filled. The store manager was a woman named Ruth, and she asked Don if he wouldn't mind waiting around until after the lunch rush. He said he wouldn't.

When the rush came, Ruth already had every worker's favorite sandwich lined up at the hoagie counter when they arrived. "This one likes a little bit of mustard, a little mayonnaise," she told Don, almost as if revealing state secrets. "And this one likes his lettuce broken, not cut up." All the wrappers had hand-drawn smiley faces on them.

The workers had little time to get their food and get back to the factory, but Ruth interjected sincere small talk as they came and went: "How's your daughter doing, Johnny?" she said. "The wife feeling any better, Stan?"

After it calmed down again, Ruth set to polishing and cleaning the equipment, getting it ready for the post-work rush.

"They're going to stop by for milk or other things to take home," she told Don. "The store has got to look its best. If it's not perfect, why, I wouldn't have them to my house if it wasn't clean. And I certainly wouldn't have them here!"

When Dick Wood finally came through the door, Don short-circuited the interview and called out: "I want to join your company," he said.

"Why is that?" Dick asked.

"There's magic here," Don said with a grin, "and I'm sure it doesn't happen all the time at every place. My job will be to help figure out what makes it happen, and what makes it not happen."

Don went on to play a crucial role in creating the playbook for winning the hearts and minds of our customers and our associates. By listening carefully to our customers and our associates, the Wawa magic has evolved to occupy that special place in the hearts of our customers. Harley-Davidson did it with motorcycles; Apple did it with iPhones. Wawa does it with convenience.

We win share of hearts through a relentless focus on three key things: weaving Wawa into the fabric of customers' lives; creating authentic and positive Wawa experiences for our customers and associates; and going the extra mile for our people, customers, and communities.

Let's look at some of the specific ways we make these three things happen.

At its core, Wawa has always been a neighborhood store, and that starts with proximity. To be part of someone's life, you need to live close by.

"We saw that and agreed to regionally clustering stores," Don says. "We would build stores in a geographic area to a point that people would get into the Wawa habit. They would tell others about the Wawa experience—and word-of-mouth can be the best marketing tool of all." Another strategy became our belief in organic growth, building stores from the ground up, not through acquisitions.

As we've already noted, that clustering strategy turned out to be a hallmark of ours. In many parts of our core areas, it's almost impossible to get where you need to go without passing one of our stores, and that has made Wawa an integral part of our customers' lives.

Frequency is the other side of Wawa's customer connection. Unlike the patrons of other popular stores, Wawa customers tend to visit our stores not once a week, but a few times a day. Very few retailers or even favorite restaurants have created that kind of repeated drop-in relationship. It's rare that you would visit a McDonald's more than one or two times a week. It's not uncommon for a Wawa customer to visit first thing in the morning for a favorite cup of coffee or breakfast item, return at lunch for a quick sandwich, and again on the way home from work or school to grab a snack or fill the gas tank.

We were also early adaptors of the *third place* concept: the idea that aside from home and work, our business is the most prominent, necessary, regular part of people's daily schedules. While that term was certainly popularized by longtime Starbucks CEO Howard Schultz, Wawa stores have been community meeting places for decades. This has overturned the old adage that absence makes the heart grow fonder. Over the years, we've learned that repetition and frequency get into the heart in a way that absence never could. Sometimes, that passion and connection our customers feel for us can lead to moments that are difficult, especially when we close a store.

Over the years, we've had to close stores that can no longer deliver the experience our customers have come to expect. We have a keen awareness that what separates successful retailers from those who haven't succeeded is the ability to change and make difficult decisions no matter how painful and emotional they may be. We recognize change is necessary and that, at times, we can't renovate or expand older stores to support our current offer. We believe retailers who don't change run the risk of going out of business.

Since 1964, we've closed 392 stores, including the entire market of Connecticut and at one point, Staten Island, New York. We weren't successful in Connecticut or Staten Island. We also lacked quality sites; moving or modernizing and enlarging our stores would have been difficult in terms of permits and zoning. And frankly, we made a few tactical mistakes, such as giving away Philadelphia Eagles football calendars in a market that was geographically and emotionally wedded to the New York Giants and New England Patriots. We exited the markets there in favor of Virginia.

In many cases, customers will let us know how much they want their Wawa to stay. Closing a store is never easy. They are decisions that tug at our heartstrings because we know that all the communities we serve become part of our extended family.

Being woven into the lives of our customers is a privilege that must be earned. It's the customer who chooses to invite us into their life. We believe, based on decades of feedback from our loyal customers, that people make Wawa part of their routine because we treat them like real people, not just customers.

Many people working in retail limit their customer interactions in order to save time and money. At most you hear the cliché "May I help you?" or the insincere "Have a nice day." At Wawa, we encourage real customer interactions, not phony, scripted ones. And by doing this, we get to really know our customers at a human level.

During my time, I also tried to follow in the goose tracks of my passionate predecessors by creating my own alter ego: the Brand Ranger. The concept of the character was my own take on the Lone Ranger. I created it to find a memorable way to encourage our associates to stay true to our brand, showing I was committed to it, even if it took being a goof to do it. I called our associateds my Brand Deputies, in charge of consistently building a brand people could trust. I would bet this approach was more effective than dropping a dry, quickly forgettable manual on their counter. I wanted to lead by example, showing by my own actions that we want our associates to have fun and be themselves with customers. Today's shoppers can see through corporate platitudes; if we want them to welcome us into their lives, we need to provide genuine, sincere human interaction, which the Brand Ranger inspires:

THE BRAND RANGER'S THEME SONG
(To the tune of Stand by Your Man)
You know that when you work at Wawa
Each day you do the best you can,
You'll have some good times,
You'll have some tough times,
Some times when it all hits the fan . . .
But still the customers expect us
To give them help and understand
They need us 'cause we
Make their lives easy
That's why they choose the Wawa brand!

Stand by your brand
So all the world will know that
They cannot live without us
They'll shout "My choice, my Wawa!"
Stand by your brand
So when they see our logo
They'll know they'll go forevermore
To a Wa—wa-ah store!
Stand by your brand
Store teams and goose together
Will soar so high across the land!
Stand by your brand!

Our strategy for winning share of hearts includes a focus on creating great experiences for our customers and associates.

Orchestrating millions of positive experiences is the ultimate goal in any retail environment. Customer experience is the sum of all experiences a customer has with a business or a brand. In a Wawa store, it can include things like sensory stimuli, human interactions, value perceptions, environmental influences, and even psychological associations. To create the optimal Wawa experience requires an understanding of the customers' views, states of mind, expectations, needs, and goals in relation to our store and our products.

At Wawa, the positive experience begins even before they get into our store with what many customers call the "hold-the-door happy chain." The chain originates with the morning's first customer. As that person is leaving, they tend to hold the door for the next person coming in. Maybe they say hello, or just nod, but either way, it feels good—a neighbor helping a neighbor. It's such a simple little gesture with a huge impact. Minutes later, we see that second customer doing the same thing for another new customer, and so on all day long—thousands of little happy gestures spreading across hundreds of stores every day.

Of course, once they come into our store we've orchestrated every sight, sound, smell, taste, and touch to show them how much we care. Our stores are built for our customers' convenience and happiness.

One of the early changes we made to improve our in-store experience was to separate the check-out line from the deli. This meant we had to hire additional people to help speed lunch orders without holding up the checkout line. It seems like an obvious adjustment now, but at the time, the rest of the industry thought we were crazy. "Double the labor costs?" they said.

The reaction from the customers, however, was different. Yes, this did double our labor costs, but more important it gave us a consistently positive experience regardless of the number of people in the store. Customers didn't have to wait, and we were happier because cars were no longer clogging up valuable parking spaces during long waits for service.

The biggest part of the Wawa experience is the food items. During our early years of growth as a food provider, we wanted—and needed—to become known for something unique in the food space, so we organized focus-group interviews to better understand what might be the unfulfilled food needs of our customers.

We liked the idea of introducing hoagies in our stores, so we convened groups of hoagie lovers to test the concept. "We're thinking of making built-to-order hoagies," the facilitator would say to a room of twenty Philadelphia hoagie aficionados.

"No, no, no," they said. "Never."

"Why's that?" the facilitator would prod.

"I have a little hoagie shop in the neighborhood that I love."

"What do you love about it?"

"The meat is sliced right before my eyes. I get to watch them build it. And I'm part of it! They'll say, 'How do you want your lettuce? Do you want it added first or last?' And I'll say, 'Please throw it on last, not first.'"

We decided to ask a different question: "What *don't* you like at the neighborhood hoagie shop?"

That produced even more answers, some of which piqued our interest.

"They're often closed when I want to go there." "They're not open around the clock." "Sometimes they run out of rolls, and sometimes the rolls aren't even fresh." "How good the hoagie is depends on who's on duty to make it." "Even the good shops are inconsistent." "If business is slow, the meats aren't as fresh as they should be."

We realized that these complaints represented opportunities. We could attack the negatives one at a time and win their hearts and stomachs.

We approached the issues in several ways:

- Wawa would be open 24/7/365.
- Wawa would build made-to-order sandwiches in front of our customers' eyes and according to how they liked them.
- Wawa's separate checkout register would speed service.
- Wawa would form a partnership with world-famous Amoroso's Baking Company to make sure fresh rolls were always available.
- Wawa would use only the freshest ingredients—a promise customers could believe because we were already known for selling lots of deli products every day.

The more committed we became to the sandwich business, the better we got at it, especially when consumers became interested in greater portion control. Hoagies, by their nature, tend to be rather large, but over time, more and more customers told us, "Your sandwiches are too big for me."

We responded the only way we know how to: "How can we help?"

"Why not make a shorter one?"

As a result, the Shorti® was born. The original full-size hoagie became the Classic,® and we added a size for kids, the Jr.® Each became a real brand customers ordered by name rather than small, medium, or large.

Trust, just as it was with our dairy, was a key competitive advantage in building our hoagie business. Trust is the underpinning of every great brand and every great company. And it can't be phony. It's got to be the real thing. Our commitment to making the best hoagies in the world earned us that trust and helped us add a powerful new component to our customer experience.

Hoagies have long been one of the iconic products most people think about first when they hear the name Wawa. It's a connection we've always been proud to boast about, despite the fact that the world's first official Hoagie Day, which was organized by Wawa's public relations manager Lori Bruce, almost didn't happen.

Here's how it came about. In 1991, Wawa worked with the Earle, Palmer Brown & Spiro ad agency and account representative Belle Gauvry to design and launch an award-winning hoagie campaign. It took the best of show award at the annual Public Relations Society of America Philadelphia chapter event and set the stage for more than two decades of hoagie celebrations.

It began with a petition drive to have the hoagie proclaimed the official sandwich of Philadelphia. Lori Bruce and Christine McCarthy, who today is Wawa's fun factory and cultural events manager, worked with a large gaggle of Wawa associates to blanket downtown Philly at an event called Super Sunday, in search of signatures for our petitions.

At the time, Ed Rendell was running for mayor. As luck would have it, Lori and Christine encountered Rendell at the event. "Mr. Rendell," they asked politely, "would you sign our petition to proclaim the hoagie the official sandwich of Philadelphia?"

"Oh, of course," he said. "I love hoagies." The campaign went on to gather 30,000 signatures in total.

Six weeks later, Rendell was elected mayor. The following spring, Wawa was preparing for the first Hoagie Day event in May, and we submitted our petition to City Hall to request a proclamation legitimizing the hoagie as the official sandwich of Philadelphia.

"We can't do that," Rendell's staff replied. "Philadelphia already has the cheese steak! Everyone knows that's our official sandwich!"

But Wawa had a crucial piece of evidence otherwise: the new mayor's own signature on a petition supporting the hoagie's preeminence. A mad search began to find the petition with Rendell's signature. "We looked for days," Lori recalls. "Oh, my God," I thought, "the entire campaign and event hinges upon this one signature!"

Once the telltale signature was found, Rendell's staff agreed to issue the proclamation. But ever the politician, Rendell found a brilliant workaround that left everyone satisfied. A proclamation named the hoagie Philadelphia's official sandwich, but added that the cheese steak would always be the City of Brotherly Love's official **hot** sandwich.

Rendell, who a decade later served two terms as governor of Pennsylvania (2003–2011), even attended the very first Hoagie Day celebration to make his endorsement official. A 500-foot hoagie was served free outside of City Hall, and rock-and-roll legend Chubby Checker performed a concert. TV stations from Philadelphia to Dallas ran coverage on the celebration. It was all about hoagies, Philadelphia . . . and Wawa.

In 1993, Rendell invited Wawa Hoagie Day to become part of the city's Welcome America! festival held during the Fourth of July weeklong festivities. Through the years, Wawa even built a Rendelli Hoagie one Hoagie Day to support early education childhood initiatives in Philadelphia. After a ten-year run in Philadelphia, Wawa took Hoagie Day on the road to Richmond, Virginia, and then to Norfolk. In 2010, Hoagie Day returned to Philadelphia as part of the Wawa Welcome America! festival where we now dedicate the event to our heroes: the military, firefighters, and police. During two decades of Hoagie Day celebrations, Wawa has served more than twenty-four miles of hoagies to hundreds of thousands and saluted numerous community organizations.

The hoagie was also the star of one of the best advertising campaigns we ever did. It was "The Symphony of the Hoagie," a unique TV campaign created in 1984 by our then marketing director, Fritz Schroeder, that used beautiful classical music playing underneath a parade of fresh hoagie ingredients. Schroeder's work won second place in that year's CLIO awards (the Oscars of the advertising world), trailing only IBM (with Charlie Chaplin) and Pepsi (with Michael Jackson), who tied for first place.

And to think—none of this would have happened if we'd

How to Make a 500-foot Hoagie

Begin with 1,000 Shorti® rolls

Then layer:
38 pounds of Italian ham
38 pounds of prosciuttini
38 pounds of Genoa salami
67 pounds of provolone cheese

Top with:
136 pounds of sliced tomatoes
60 pounds of sliced onions
60 pounds of shredded iceberg lettuce
2 pounds of oregano
2 pounds (6 gallons) of oil

Add:
A *huge* dash of salt and pepper
90 pounds of hoagie wrap
Number of Wawa chefs required: 200

Serves: More than 1,000 people in less than thirty minutes
Total weight: 651 pounds!

followed the advice of the people in that first focus group and given up on the idea of ever offering fresh-made hoagies at Wawa!

. . . . .

Just as we agonized before we added the hoagie to our product offerings, we debated intensely about the possible impact of selling fuel to the Wawa customer experience. That debate included one simple but important question: What to call our brand of gasoline? We conducted research and encountered a number of people who thought we shouldn't call our fuel product "Wawa gasoline," thinking that, because we had Wawa hoagies and Wawa coffee, putting the same name on gasoline might create a bad impression.

We tested names like "Golden Goose Gasoline" and "Flying Goose Gasoline." But other customers said, "Look, you're Wawa. You've been in the dairy business for a hundred years. You're in the coffee business. You're in the hoagie business. If it's good, put your name on it." Eventually, we agreed, and decided to keep it simple and call it Wawa gasoline. No one has ever had a problem with it.

Our experience has shown that there isn't always a clear path to winning hearts, but careful planning and listening to customers can guide us in the right direction.

Our third strategy for winning share of heart is all about going the extra mile for our stakeholders.

It's hard to believe, but the commonplace marketing concept of *customer satisfaction* has never been big at Wawa. To us, satisfaction is the lowest level of experience. To get into the heart, we need to go further, beyond satisfaction into the realm of delight.

In his bestselling book, *212: The Extra Degree*, Samuel L. Parker uses a simple metaphor to create a wonderful image of the power of extra effort. He observed that at 211 degrees, water is hot. But at 212 degrees, water turns to steam, and steam can power a locomotive. He inspires everyone to go that one extra degree, and create meaningful and lasting change. The book provides many examples in which the difference between first place and second is merely millimeters or tenths of a second.

You can only get to delight by going the extra mile. Believe me, if you've ever received an unexpected hug from eighty-nine-year-old associate "Grandmom Pat" Sacco at store 3 in Brookhaven, Pennsylvania, you understood what going the extra mile truly means. More than that, you probably told everybody about it: "I stopped by and saw Grandmom Pat, and she gave me a hug like she always does every morning with her coffee."

Customers filled the store on the occasion of Grandmom Pat's eighty-ninth birthday, but it wasn't the celebration that she treasured the most. It was, instead, the daily connection she made with her customers. They, too, valued the human moments and the extra effort she puts into everything she does. Is there any advertisement that's better than that?

Thankfully, at Wawa we are blessed with a team of associates who go the extra mile by spreading good cheer and happiness on a daily basis. Our people passionately want to change the world, one smile and one cup of coffee at a time.

Naturally, it has helped to have people like Don Price, who considered it his job to incessantly excite and encourage our team. That's why, for much of his time with the company, he held the title of Minister of the Magic.

"Even the part-timer understands that they can create that magic," he said.

In one way, Don was following in the footsteps of Grahame Wood. That day he came in for his job interview the store manager, Ruth, told Don a story about a personal note she found addressed to her in the store's back office:

Dear Ruth,

I'm glad to hear your bowling score is improving . . .

Grahame

Don became a believer in handwritten notes to our associates. Corporate memos are fine. But taking the time to write something personal is going the extra mile. For the next twenty years, it was a real mark of success for someone to receive a "Don-O-Gram." Many of Don's handwritten notes can be found today, framed and prominently hung in the homes of the recipients.

Wawa Tags and Slogans through the Years

Paid advertising has always played second fiddle to word of mouth when it comes to spreading the good news about Wawa. But ads have had a role in helping to build our business over the past several decades. Here are some of our favorite tags and slogans used to promote Wawa products through the years. How many do you remember?

1950s: Bottled Fresh in the Country . . . Serving Your Neighbors . . . Why Not You?

1960s: Mama I Luv Wawa

1970s: People on the Go—Go to Wawa Food Markets

1980s: We do it just a little bit better: Wawa

1990s: One great taste after another

1990s: Mornin', Noon And Nite, Wawa Does It Right

1990s: Go to Wawa when you're hot, hot, hot

2002–2005: My choice. My Wawa.

2005–present: Gottahava Wawa

Similarly, Don publicized our associates' work in winning the hearts of customers and whole communities by overseeing an ongoing effort to shoot and gather photos of special events, including milestone celebrations or just exciting store visits, which are displayed on walls throughout our offices and distributed to customers, associates, and families. Currently, Wawa has an archive of more than 100,000 photos that manifest its culture and reflect our associates' passion for the business, memorializing everything from ribbon-cutting ceremonies to charity events. Parts of the collection have been cross-indexed by associate names and events. These efforts, some Wawa associates say, are "the wind beneath our wings."

Thanks to our consistent efforts to practice these three strategies—becoming part of our customers' lives, creating great experiences, and going the extra mile—Wawa has been winning hearts for more than a century. The Wawa brand has had a halo over it since the days of milkmen delivering pure dairy products door to door, and the same halo continues to shine today—as it will for decades to come.

Everyday Wawa associates go above and beyond for customers and communities, not because they have to, but because they care.

CHAPTER 10

Community as Family

The community spirit is evident internally, too. At Wawa, when a store faces a natural disaster or a personnel difficulty, the manager can count on the Wawa flock to provide support until the store is fully functional. Managers came from hundreds of miles away to help clean storefronts and do whatever else was necessary after Hurricane Isabel smashed into the Virginia area in 2003. ("Wawa" is a Native American word for Canada goose, and employees often point to the cooperative migratory habits of geese as an inspiration for their sense of community.)

—Neeli and Venkat Bendapudi, "Creating the Living Brand,"
Harvard Business Review, May 2005

From our earliest days, Wawa's philosophy has been to not only serve but also lead in the communities where we operate. Since opening our first convenience store in 1964, our community relationships have been at the heart of who we are—from championing important causes to in-store fundraising to volunteering at community events. Through the years we've focused on supporting causes that have the most significant impact on our communities, including the areas of children's and family health, hunger, and everyday heroes (firefighters, police, and the military). Serving others has always been part of our DNA. As an example, Dick Wood's father helped Children's Hospital in Philadelphia grow and expand into an internationally recognized institution. But what makes Wawa extra special is the fact that we've become more than just a business. We're also an integral part of the towns and neighborhoods we serve.

One way to illustrate this reality is through the story of a single Wawa associate—just one of the many wonderful people I was privileged to work with during my years at the company—and the connection he helped to build between Wawa and the American Red Cross.

Harry McHugh, who came to Philadelphia from Ireland to go to school and play soccer, joined Wawa in information technology and eventually conquered real estate and store operations. No one ever had a bigger heart for our business, or our community, than Harry, as demonstrated by his commitment to the American Red Cross of Southeastern Pennsylvania. Under his influence, we probably donated more blood to the American Red Cross than any other company in Philadelphia. In 2012, the Wawa team hosted over a hundred blood drives chainwide and collected a total of 4,624 units of blood. Since each unit of blood can help save three lives, Wawa associates have helped save 13,872 lives in the communities we serve.

Harry took a personal interest in the Red Cross more than four decades ago, serving for many years on the local chapter of the organization's board of directors and even as its chairman. Through his commitment, Wawa became an ardent and highly visible supporter of this great community organization.

"Wawa is *the* largest corporate donor that we have, not one of the largest that we have," says Judge Renée Cardwell Hughes, CEO of the Philadelphia-based group. "It's a function of sharing the same values of really being committed to the community, being part of the community and not being separate from the community. When you look at a Wawa store, their associates live in the community. Wawa is committed to the health and welfare of the community."

Our current CEO, Chris Gheysens, followed Harry onto the board and already chairs the Red Cross House Program Committee.

Wawa supports all Red Cross fundraisers, including the Red Ball, the Cup (a golf tournament), and the annual Red Cross 5K Walk/Run. In 2013, as a holiday gift to motivate the staff after a really challenging year in terms of disasters, Wawa gave every Red Cross staff member a gift card.

Wawa is a major part of the Red Cross's feeding plan in major disasters. "We had an apartment fire that displaced sixty families in March 2013," Renée says. "It was a big, big, massive fire. Literally on the way to the fire, a Red Cross volunteer stopped at a Wawa store and was given emergency supplies. She stopped in her Red Cross gear and said, 'We're setting up a shelter at XYZ location.' Wawa provided breakfast for everyone."

The Wawa manager on duty made that decision without calling a supervisor or corporate headquarters and it was the right thing, in our culture, to have done.

"They're all empowered to do that," Renée says.

So wherever we have a disaster, we know we can go to
a Wawa and get the supplies that we need to ensure we can

take care of the families. It's really a seamless relationship.
When Hurricane Irene hit, we got a call from Wawa saying,
"The authorities are getting ready to close the bridges. What
do you need before that happens?" Another time they called
and said, "I've got a load of water and bread products that
I want to deliver to you before transportation is shut down."
So as much as we call Wawa, they are proactively thinking
about us. For us, that is an incredible relationship. We have
a lot of companies that are really good to us, but I'll tell you
in no uncertain terms there is no one that has a relationship
with us like Wawa.

Wawa is a leader and it sets the tone for other companies
in Philadelphia. I'm frequently asked, "What is Wawa doing?
Is Wawa supporting this?" And for us, the answer is always
"Yes!" because there really isn't anything we're involved in
that Wawa doesn't come to the table to support.

When faced with a different kind of disaster—the terrorist attacks on September 11, 2001—we moved quickly to offer our customers a way to reach out to their fellow Americans. Once again, the American Red Cross Disaster Relief Fund was the clear choice.

Our printer, PrintArt from Egg Harbor, NJ, worked around the clock to produce easels for an in-store fundraising campaign that featured bar-coded coupons in denominations of $1, $2, or $5, and we made them available at every register, in every Wawa store by Friday, September 14, to give customers a way to donate, matching a portion of customer gifts donated to support the relief effort. We were amazed when, on Monday, September 17, our customers surpassed $500,000 in donations. And donations showed no sign of waning. Some from corporations, some from children's piggy banks.

From every corner of the Wawa family, customers and associates gave from the heart.

Afterward, comments about this program poured in from associates and customers. Our associates at store 84 wrote: "We did not want to wait for our coupons to arrive, so we put a jar on our counter and started to collect donations earlier. It was something that made us feel a little better after four days and so many tears. We wish we could turn tears into dollars, you would have to match $100,000 so much earlier. Our prayers go out to so many." They signed the message "Wawa Store 84. Proud to be Americans. Proud to work for Wawa."

The employees of a Financial Services Corporation in Chadds Ford, Pennsylvania, wrote: "I know that we missed out on our money being doubled by your company, but we decided to send it to you anyway to be sure that it went to the people in need of it in New York and Washington. We appreciate your efforts in all of this. Thank you for allowing us to be a part of it."

When Mother Nature challenges us, the Wawa team is at its best. The October 2012 arrival of Hurricane Sandy—Superstorm Sandy, as it will be long remembered—was no exception.

We never before faced such a powerful storm in the Delaware Valley and the Northeast, one that was ultimately responsible for causing deaths, widespread terror, and tens of billions of dollars in damage. Sandy was the storm of the century, bringing flooding, devastating winds, and severe coastal impact, leaving millions in its wake without power.

At Wawa, we will best remember Sandy by the response of our associate team, and the ways in which our associates worked tirelessly to support their communities and their friends and neighbors. As soon as Hurricane Sandy appeared on a collision course with the Northeast, we did our best to prepare for the anticipated severity of the storm. We'd learned a lot from past experiences with community disasters, both ours and others'.

One of our most memorable first experiences with a storm of epic proportions was the blizzard of 1993. Nearly two feet of snow fell in some places, and a six-foot storm surge occurred in others. Hurricane winds, volatile icy conditions, and stinging arctic temperatures paralyzed the Mid-Atlantic, shutting down roads, airports, public transportation, and malls.

While most of the East Coast remained trapped indoors, Wawa associates did their best to keep stores open. It was a story with many heroes as associates stayed in motels near their stores to avoid having to close. Others plowed through the blizzard in four-wheel-drive vehicles to provide transportation.

All in all, Wawa associates made every effort to remain open for those who needed them. Stores made sandwiches on hot dog rolls when they ran out of bread, doing what they could to serve the responders and community members counting on them.

KYW-TV CBS 3 reporter Walt Hunter broadcast live in front of store 213 in Upper Darby, better known that day as "the Wawa community center." The Wawa call center never closed, remaining open the entire time for store support, at one point helped by Dick Wood, who walked from his home to Red Roof to help answer phones.

The next week, T-shirts were printed with the slogan IT RAN BECAUSE OF ME—DURING THE BLIZZARD OF '93 and distributed to Wawa associates who displayed the "commitment of the century" during the "storm of the century." At least, that's what people called it until the next set of big ones came along. And boy, did they. In 1994, we experienced eleven straight weeks of ice storms and in 1996, a record-setting 32-inch blizzard. But there were other disasters, too.

We'd actually committed a misstep in the wake of 9/11. Right after the attacks, gas prices were highly volatile. We were new to the fuel business at that time, having just launched in Virginia. That horrible day was crazy from a cost standpoint. Most retailers in Virginia raised their prices. We did, too, though not to profit from the tragedy. It was simply that wholesale prices made such an exorbitant jump and spiked. Some stores shut down because they were flat out of gas, and then people really panicked.

We quickly realized we'd made a mistake. We shouldn't have raised our gas prices. Within days, Harry McHugh, Vice President of Operations, drove to Virginia and apologized for the way we'd handled the crisis. We took a big short-term hit in the Washington, DC–area media. The next week we made a large donation to the Red Cross—$250,000—and took prices down.

We learned something about dealing with disasters from the 9/11 experience. We were also better prepared for Hurricane Sandy because of our experience during Hurricane Irene in August 2011.

During Irene, we overreacted because of the hype preceding the storm. We transmitted a planned shutdown decision to all stores in the affected areas. They all closed at 8:00 p.m. the night the storm approached.

However, it was not as big an event as we expected. The next day, Sal Mattera and I bluntly admitted to our associates: "We closed too many, too soon."

One of the newspapers in our market area picked up on our strategic error and published a cartoon with the tagline YOU KNOW IT MUST HAVE BEEN A DISASTER. THE WAWA WAS CLOSED.

People were beyond disbelief that we closed our doors, and we were criticized harshly for it. Along the shore, they criticized us because we boarded up, which we'd never done before. Residents who were evacuated were shocked to see our doors closed when they anxiously stopped by fill up their gas tanks.

In our defense, we didn't have a lot of previous experience with hurricanes in Philadelphia and South Jersey. By contrast, Wawa is known for facing blizzards and snowstorms with impunity. We don't shut down under any circumstances for those.

Having learned from Hurricane Irene, when natural disasters threaten our communities we now aim to be the last to close and the first to reopen. Our associates feel a social and civic responsibility to be present, even though the problems at their own homes may be severe. They will put their own needs aside in many cases to come in and keep their stores open.

Superstorm Sandy had Wawa written all over it. It came right over our market area. But because we have customers and associates with such big hearts, Wawa rallied to the occasion.

Stories of Wawa associates reaching out to their friends and neighbors in the days following Sandy's destructive power in October and November 2012 are now legendary. More than any other episode during my tenure, that time was a sterling example of our view that our community is our family. Here are a few examples of our associates and our organization shining in their finest hour:

- Upon news of our closing, our associates locked up store 223 on Bullens Lane in Woodlyne, Pennsylvania, and were in their cars leaving the lot when a Red Cross vehicle pulled in and one of the team said, "We can't operate the community shelter because we don't have any hot food." The Wawa associates got out of their cars, went back into the store, and prepared enough hot food to take back to the shelter and serve everyone who would have to stay through the night until other provisions could be arranged.
- During the storm, a call came in to Red Roof from one of the stores on Long Beach Island, New Jersey. Several associates attached to that store had their houses washed out to sea. Yet they kept the store

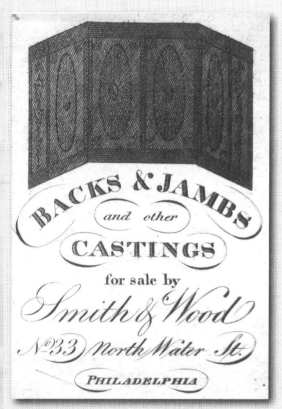

BACKS & JAMBS
and other
CASTINGS
for sale by
Smith & Wood
No 33 North Water St.
PHILADELPHIA

Smith and Wood built a foundry in Millville, New Jersey where they made cast iron fire backs, stove plates, and pipes.

Supplying citizens with potable water was an important responsibility of city governments. Philadelphia's water works was an engineering marvel and used pipe from Millville Furnace.

FAIRMOUNT PARK, PHILADELPHIA.
Photographed by James Cremer, 18 South Eighth Street, Philadelphia.

R.D. Wood built a new foundry in Millville and, in 1856, constructed a cotton mill. The manufacturing complex grew to include a bleachery and dye works.

A decorative iron fence from Millville Furnace is shown in front of the Wood family house. The building is now home to the Millville Historical Society.

Horse drawn delivery van pictured in front of 32nd and Woodland Avenue depot. Milk from the country arrived at Wawa's refrigerated depot in West Philadelphia via railroad and, from there, was delivered to customers.

Wawa Dairy Farms opened in 1902 to sell doctor certified milk from purebred Guernsey cows.

In 1929, at a cost of $250,000, Wawa built an ultra-modern plant that housed two dairies—one for certified raw milk and the other for pasteurized product.

World War II veteran Tom Summers delivered Wawa milk in the mid 1950s. He and other milkmen were the face of the company in the community. Wawa milkmen could be trusted with the keys to customers' homes so that milk could be placed directly in their refrigerators.

Long-time employee Ethel Tyers is shown in the mid 1990s at the half gallon filler monitoring, sealing, and date stamping milk cartons.

Martin Kane Photograph

Grahame Wood transformed his family's company by consolidating resources, focusing on the dairy's reputation for quality products, and entering a new business— convenience stores.

Wawa opened its first convenience store in Folsom, Delaware County, Pennsylvania on April 16, 1964.

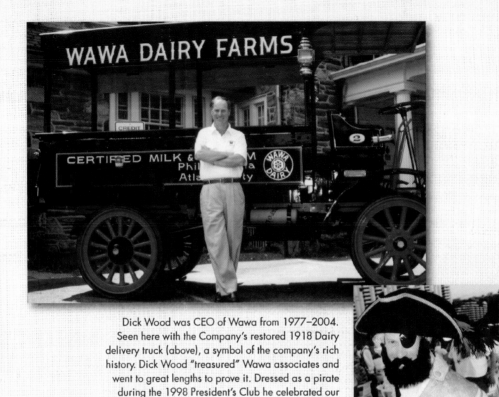

Dick Wood was CEO of Wawa from 1977–2004.
Seen here with the Company's restored 1918 Dairy
delivery truck (above), a symbol of the company's rich
history. Dick Wood "treasured" Wawa associates and
went to great lengths to prove it. Dressed as a pirate
during the 1998 President's Club he celebrated our
top general managers and led a treasure hunt (right).

Howard Stoeckel, Dick Wood, and Jim Bluebello at one of Wawa's
new fuel stores (below). Dick was the driving force behind Wawa
building bigger stores and adding gasoline to our offer. New ways
to simplify our customers' daily lives.

Not everything worked the first time around. We opened Wawa kitchens in 1968 featuring meatloaf and fried chicken. Just slightly ahead of their time, the kitchens were all closed within a year or two.

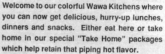

Welcome to our colorful Wawa Kitchens where you can now get delicious, hurry-up lunches, dinners and snacks. Either eat here or take home in our special "Take Home" packages which help retain that piping hot flavor.

An "Umbrelli from the Deli"—Another one of Wawa's fabulous flops. A promotion for our deli that failed but we learned from it—you can't count on the weather and it did nothing for our fresh food image.

One short-term failure that ultimately turned successful was fuel. In the late 70s and early 1980s, we had a few stores with one or two gas pumps, but shut most of them down by 1985. In 1996, we tried again with a bigger and more focused offer and this time succeeded.

The tradition of private ownership of Wawa began with its origins as a family business. Today, the Wood family continues to have the majority ownership interest in Wawa. They meet annually to stay informed about the business.

Wawa associates celebrate ownership month. They currently own more than 38% of Wawa through an Employee Stock Ownership Plan (ESOP).

Harry McHugh epitomized the servant leader. Whether visiting stores on Christmas Day to thank associates, or championing blood drives for the Red Cross, Harry's dedication to service helped demonstrate Wawa's six core values.

Wawa's Associates in Need fund (AIN) shows our associates they are part of our family and deserve the personal support family members would give to each other.

Wawa's six core values define us. Here, our mailroom team displays icons illustrating the values: Value People, Delight Customers, Embrace Change, Do Things Right, Do The Right Thing, and Passion for Winning.

Creating a family environment is part of valuing people at Wawa. Harriet Pearson celebrates her 90th birthday with fellow associates and customers at the Wawa store in Cinnaminson, New Jersey where she worked for fourteen years.

Don Price our "Minister of the Magic" leads Christine McCarthy and the rest of the Prize Patrol to a celebration to recognize store achievement.

Our Values Storybook is published every year to highlight the best of our values and culture. Since 2007, the Values Program has received more than 28,000 thousand values submissions and stories from associates.

On July 4th, hundreds of Wawa volunteers pass out flags, hats, and refreshing beverages to the crowds that gather in Philadelphia to celebrate America's birthday during Wawa Welcome America!

Ye Haw! It's Howard Stoeckel as Brand Ranger—champion of the Wawa brand.

When we traveled 1,000 miles to expand into Florida, our values traveled with us. We were humbled by the number of customers who drove for miles and stood shoulder to shoulder to wait patiently for their first taste of Wawa in Florida.

Our Wellness Journey involves embracing change and a personal commitment. James Broglin (left), from store 360 in Sewell, NJ had the help of fellow associate, Jim Casper (right) who encouraged him on his journey to a healthier lifestyle.

Wawa is committed to continuous change and innovation. In 2010 the coffee areas at every store were redesigned, replacing glass coffee pots with energy-efficient, branded thermals.

Committed to doing things right, Wawa's product development teams and operations engineers tested espresso equipment for years before selecting the perfect choice to support Wawa's launch of hot, iced, and frozen specialty beverages in 2011.

Since 2002, Mandy Lain on the Internal Care team has sent thousands of care packages to the troops serving overseas. Mandy's initiative is confirmation of Wawa's dedication to do the right thing.

Chris Gheysens presents a check to the American Red Cross Disaster Relief Fund. Through Wawa's partnership with the Red Cross, Wawa is able to help its neighbors quickly and effectively in times of crisis.

With our Florida design, Wawa strove to create a fresh and inviting exterior that included outside seating in the "Sunshine State".

Wawa served a mile-long hoagie on Independence Mall in honor of Wawa Hoagie Day, an annual event that celebrates our communities, customers, and associates and pays tribute to Philadelphia's official sandwich.

Wawa associates are passionate about supporting causes. Many teams support the Special Olympic Polar Plunges—to raise funds and awareness of the needs of others.

Wawa's 50th Anniversary celebration on April 16, 2014, was a wonderful manifestation of 50 years in the retail business, celebrating our values, culture, and our relationship with almost 700 store communities in the mid-Atlantic states and Florida.

Wawa's 50th anniversary milestone generated numerous print and broadcast stories. Reporters wrote about the special relationship between Wawa and the community of its origin, Greater Philadelphia.

Philadelphia Mayor Michael Nutter and former Pennsylvania Governor Ed Rendell joined Wawa in introducing The Wawa Foundation for the first time. Five $50,000 grant checks were distributed to causes in support of areas focusing on health, hunger, and everyday heroes.

Former Governor Rendell is presented with a giant version of the "Rendelli," a throwback to the original hoagie named for him when he was mayor. Mayor Nutter is presented with a namesake hoagie created for him – turkey on wheat with veggie toppings – the "Nutter Classic."

Florida associates are excited to serve residents a fresh and appetizing experience. They show dedication and commitment, becoming great brand ambassadors in not just communicating and promoting our culture, but in finding and hiring new generations of people who share the same values.

Wawa opens its 25th Wawa store in Florida on August 29, 2013 – just outside the Orlando International airport. Fuel was priced at $2.99 gallon next door to "competitors" notorious for having the highest gasoline prices in the country. Thanks to Orlando's Mayor Buddy Dyer's support and circumstances with local competitors, it was the highest profile to date with media coverage garnering more than 1 million local viewers with 50-plus news stories related to our opening.

Wawa associates proudly support charitable events, such as walks or community events. They are fiercely passionate about the causes they support.

Wawa's kicks off their grand opening celebration of its 50th store in Florida on September 18, 2014 at 4100 E. Colonial Drive, Orlando, Florida. Customers, associates, locals, and Wawa officials cut the ribbon to declare the store offically open!

The Wawa Foundation has become one of the most important vehicles to enable us to live our values and fulfill lives every day by building stronger communities. On Wawa Day we spotlight the work of the foundation and honor some of our charity partners.

On Wawa Day we thank our customers for millions of unforgettable moments.

Our associates are the most important part of our support to annual events such as the Philadelphia Komen Race for the Cure.

Celebrating the summer season with value, t-shirts, decorations, and more, Hoagiefest ho become one of our most beloved and iconic campaigns.

New Connections is an annual "listening tour" to share our purpose and hear the voice of associates.

5-Star Service Awards honor the top stores for in-store excellence and customer appreciation based on customer feedback. The celebrations honor our "superheroes of service."

The Wawa brand and family like atmosphere is unique as customers often share their special moments with us.

open as long as they could until the fire chief contacted our manager, Tom Howard, to request assistance and products for the hundreds of emergency responders addressing critical needs. We told them, "Take whatever you need." They salvaged water, soda, juice, energy bars, cereal, canned soup, toiletries, cleaning supplies, paper plates, cups, and utensils and gave them to responders.

- "Wawa saved the town" are the words Parsippany Mayor Barberio utters every time he regales a school group, Boy Scout troop, or community member about a pivotal event that occurred in Parsippany last year in the aftermath of Superstorm Sandy. It all began when Scott Kent, a Wawa area manager received an urgent phone call at 8:00 a.m. from one of his general managers, Robert Taubenslag, who had been contacted by members of the Office of Emergency Management in Parsippany. "Our water system is up and running on diesel generators," they said, "but we only have enough fuel on hand to last until 7:00 p.m. tonight. If we do not get fuel, we have to shut down the generators, which will stop the water going out to thousands of homes and businesses and potentially shut down the sewer system in five other towns as well." Scott Kent flew into action and contacted Wawa's strategic fuel team to see what they could do . . . and fast! Together the Wawa strategic fuel team used every avenue to locate and transport the precious diesel, and divert a Wawa diesel shipment headed to a Wawa store to support the cause. At 6:00 p.m. that night, with less than hour before the town's water and sewer system would have been shut down, a Wawa diesel shipment arrived in Parsippany, just in the nick of time, keeping the water system going. Mayor Barberio will never forget how Wawa turned what could have been a major crisis into an event that cemented Wawa's commitment to be a good neighbor.

- Tom Di Stefano from our internal care department frequently drove from Red Roof in Delaware County to severely affected areas served by Wawa and provided cash and gift cards so our associates could get meals or even diapers for their little ones. Internal care even helped displaced associates find rental homes when necessary. We also took care of those associates who weren't able to work, either because they had family responsibilities or their stores were badly damaged. The key was no red tape.

- April M. Ferrante-Church is a Wawa general manager. In the wake of the storm, she and her team collected toys and gifts for Operation Santa and distributed them in Brick, New Jersey, an area hard hit by Sandy. Nobody at Red Roof told April to do that. In fact, she put a box in the store and collected toys, which typically we wouldn't authorize. But she was so personally compelled and empowered that she came up with that on her own. And we couldn't complain about the initiative she demonstrated and the goodwill her individual act of charity inspired.

We received any number of letters from our customers saying, "I may have only been an occasional Wawa customer, but now I'm a Wawa customer forever because you were there for me."

When we had long lines of people filling their gas canisters with diesel to take home and run their portable generators, our associates were out there talking to the customers, giving out food samples, and making a pleasant experience out of a difficult circumstance. It was Wawa at its finest.

Scott Kent puts it this way:

> *Our people rise to the occasion when the community*
> *needs us the most. Wawa team members balanced dealing*

with their own adversity—so many of our associates that
worked for the stores impacted by Sandy had significant
situations at home. Loss of power, loss of homes,
devastation, yet they still stayed connected to the business,
trying to balance out serving their community, their friends,
their neighbors—people they viewed as just as important as
trying to take care of themselves.

It was just huge for our brand. I call it "Sandy love."
People found the stores during Sandy, fell in love with us,
appreciated what we did and stayed with us.

Boy, did people follow us on social media during the storm and its aftermath, trying to determine which stores were closed and when they would reopen. We had the second highest day of traffic in our history—2,832,869 million hits on Wawa.com. We made a $100,000 contribution to Red Cross disaster relief as a company, but through charity donation scan campaigns that utilize bar code technology to ensure financial integrity, our store associates collected an additional $297,000 in nine days, a wonderful achievement.

Of course, we experienced our own problems during the historic storm. We didn't realize that some stores didn't have the proper external hookups for generators. With no electricity, and phone lines under water, we had an extremely difficult time communicating. Unlike Irene, we probably waited too long to close stores, and should have given our associates more time to get out of harm's way.

Still, on the whole, we have a lot to be proud of at Wawa when looking back on our response to Sandy. I think our associates set a wonderful example of what it means to be good corporate citizens. And in the process they created an even stronger bond between our brand and the people we serve. It's a story that illustrates the Wawa way at its very best.

Howard Stoeckel, with his oversized crayon, inspires the Wawa team to "Think Big."

CHAPTER 11

The Bird's-Eye View

Store managers are expected to make each Wawa "part of the community" and impress regulars who will come in five times a week or more. . . . Repeat customers bring up the employees and say things like "Your people like each other, they have fun and work as a team, and when we come in to the store we feel part of that."

—Rob Walker, "Convenience Cult" *New York Times,* July 30, 2006

It has become a Wawa tradition for the CEO to produce a list of principles that reflects his business focus and priorities for the company.

This chapter is about the ten priorities that guided my own eight years as CEO of Wawa. Most of these guiding principles aren't ideas I simply made up; they're ideas I inherited from past generations of Wawa leaders and identified in my experiences with our associates and customers. I was proud to adopt them as my signature messages, which I reinforced at every opportunity.

BUILT FROM THE BOTTOM UP

Grahame Wood and Dick Wood were extremely empathetic toward store associates. "They are my number one customers," Dick would say.

As CEO, I always tried to live up to his example. Dick was a champion of our store tour process in which every executive, every month, went out and spent a minimum of a day in a single store or group of stores, the latter with an area manager. We would visit as many as fifteen stores, talking to each and every associate. We wanted to discover hidden issues, document their concerns, and uncover all the good things that were happening as well. We published reports after these tours, and management would gather for a half day every month to review the findings so we could improve life at the store level.

We've found this is simply the most effective way to maintain Wawa's success. Where we have great store managers, we always have great stores. A store chain is like a sports team: Everyone has to execute at his or her position. When they do, the team wins championships.

This point of view should be commonplace, but I've found it's unusual. Many companies build teams around free agents, high-priced talent, and big egos. We build teams around ordinary people, and we want everyone to play their position, be a team player, and contribute to something bigger than themselves.

Historically, we've always paid our managers quite well compared to standard industry rates. We believe that our general managers, in particular, should be compensated above industry averages, because theirs is such a demanding job.

We're a company that never sleeps, one that combines three businesses—convenience, food service, and fuel—on one piece of property serving as many as 25,000 to 30,000 customers a week. Our businesses are higher volume than most quick-service restaurants in terms of food service, certainly much higher than other convenience stores, and much higher than other gas retailers. Therefore, our more than six hundred general managers are absolutely critical to our success.

We refer to them as *intrapreneurs*. They have the entrepreneurial spirit, but they express it within the Wawa system. We provide the resources, we build the stores, and we provide the guidelines, the culture, and a tremendous amount of support in the form of bonuses, incentives, and educational programs.

In 1992, for instance, we implemented a store general manager bonus program called Controllable Gross Margin to encourage our people to think like entrepreneurs. It shares profits from aspects of the business that they can control—sales, gross profit, labor, shrinkage, and spoilage—and pays a bonus based on improvement. That has ended up being a powerful incentive that created unprecedented accountability at the store level and fostered the intrapreneurship we believed in.

We also started a system called Strong Store Leaders. Now, in addition to the GM, each store has an assistant general manager and a fresh-food manager. In the fuel stores there's a fuel manager, and many stores also have an inventory merchandise manager. We don't think there's any convenience retailer in the country that has this depth of bench strength or that is spending as much money as we are on its store leadership structure. It pays dividends because these people *are* the Wawa brand.

Knowing we need a steady flow of talent to fill this array of leadership positions, we've also created a system for hiring, training, and developing people that is unique to Wawa.

When I first joined Wawa in 1987, we didn't have many formal training programs in place. We had extremely high employee turnover, complicated by a tight employment market. Unemployment was low, our wages were okay but not great, and the image of a convenience retailer back in those days was so-so. Few school kids said, "When I grow up, I want to work at a convenience store!" In particular, we were having trouble keeping store managers.

To address these issues, we created something we called Camp Wawa, based in the Pocono Mountains at a rustic resort called the Sterling Inn. This five-day leadership program was all about helping our people find their uniqueness and recognize their potential for leading others, for better understanding the Wawa culture, for better understanding how to empower people, and for learning how to take their business to the next level.

At first, many of the participants didn't want to drive three hours to the mountains and be away from their families for days. They didn't know what they were getting into. There were a lot of unknowns because we'd never done anything of this nature before.

But by the middle of the week, people didn't want to leave. And by the end of the week, many were emotional about going home because it had been such a wonderful learning experience they could take back to their stores.

Camp Wawa was so successful that it encouraged us to build additional training programs for our budding leaders, resulting in what is now called Wawa University.

Wawa University is a way to reinvest in our associates, many of whom have not been to college, and train them for handling increasingly complex store operations. It's the first academic experience outside of high school for many of our people. For their benefit, we want to create a real-life college environment.

We first set it up on the campus of West Chester University, located near Red Roof. We rented their facilities, put associates in their dormitories, used their classrooms, and created a faculty consisting of West Chester University professors and some of our own leadership team, including Jim Shortall as our first "dean." The curriculum presented the fundamentals of business: Business Management 101, Human Resource Management 101, and Marketing Management 101.

Learning the Wawa Way

Wawa is an organization built from the ground up—and that's why we provide one of the most extensive training and education programs for associates in our industry.

A customer service associate must complete over sixty-five hours of both on-the-job training and computer-based instruction to become proficient at all positions in a Wawa fuel store. Classes include everything from how to use a fire extinguisher to how to keep the store safe for customers with disabilities.

An associate who wants to become a shift manager must complete ten different on-line classes before they can even register for two additional days of classroom training.

Wawa store management personnel experience an average of over twenty hours of webinars, on-the-job training, and classroom training over a three-week period as part of the orientation process. One of the first classes is on Wawa's core purpose, its six core values, and the company's vision for the future.

General managers attend a weeklong "Servant Leadership Development Program" which focuses on the company's servant leadership framework and leadership competencies. The program explores company culture and effective leadership practices.

Wawa corporate associates have over three weeks of training to take on their journey up the corporate ladder. The last class covers servant leadership—the core idea upon which leadership at Wawa is based.

In the years since then, Wawa University has evolved and grown. We've relocated it to a Wawa facility adjacent to our original dairy. We now partner with a number of universities to bring a vast array of college courses to our people, including both business classes (geared especially toward Wawa's practices) and liberal arts classes. Immaculata University, Saint Joseph's University, and others come to us, making it even easier and more convenient for our people to get a proper and life-enhancing education. The goal is a bachelor of arts or a bachelor of science degree—a real, universally recognized diploma made possible through our affiliation with Immaculata. It's just that we make it convenient.

Many of our mid-level managers attend our executive program with Saint Joseph's. Our main contact there is Richard George, chair and professor of food marketing at Saint Joseph's University's Haub School of Business in Philadelphia. Rich has a special history with Wawa—he was actually a customer in store 1 not long after it opened in 1964. He's been a customer and a fan ever since.

"Wawa values education," Rich says. "They walk the talk."

The student body at Wawa University has a number of unusual characteristics. The gray matter in our thirty-, forty- or fifty-year-old Wawa associates going to college, sometimes for the first time, is no better or worse than that of the eighteen-year-olds attending straight out of high school. Their motivation, however, is much higher because they understand better than most youngsters how important an education is and recognize immediately how to apply their lessons to the challenges of real life.

The results speak for themselves in countless stories of people who have improved their lives, careers, and certainly the company through these programs—too many to fit in these pages.

In fact, this led us to create an entirely new department centered around recognizing the accomplishments of our people. We call it internal care, and I've already mentioned its activities several times. The idea behind internal care is simple. Wonderful things are happening in every business, every day, that we should know about, read about, recognize, and share with our people. Internal care makes it happen. We now create recognition cards and pins, and ultimately celebrate three thousand people a year.

Wawa is about great products and friendly service, but even more, it's about building people with the ability and drive to make their dreams come true.

FOLLOW YOUR DREAMS

Plenty of men and women smarter than I and better educated never achieved their potential. In most cases, the reason for their disappointment was their lack of a dream.

Like individuals, companies must have dreams. We must have a destination and a plan to get there. If we can dream it, we can make it come true with hard work, with the right people sharing our dream, and the resources for the journey.

A dream isn't about dollars and cents. It's about a higher calling. It's about what we want to be. It's about what's important and what's relevant to the people around us.

If you focus only on numbers, you'll achieve short-term results. But when you focus on a dream, you can travel to unknown and uncharted places, accomplishing things far greater than you might have imagined possible.

Most important, dreams must inspire and align everyone in the organization. I've met a lot of executives with great strategies who didn't quite inspire because they couldn't articulate a clear, crisp vision. At Wawa, we've always tried to bring simplicity to our vision, using descriptors and storytelling to make it come to life and to give it breadth. If we don't connect our associates on the front line to our dream, it will never become a reality.

And what is the Wawa dream?

We believe we are already one of the world's most appetizing convenience retailers, and we prove that by having major market share wherever we compete with globally recognized brands. The next evolution of what we call our Blue Ocean journey is to become fast-casual to go with world-class convenience.

The fastest-growing segment of food is fast-casual. The restaurant industry is basically comprised of three segments:

Quick service: McDonald's, Burger King, Wendy's, Carl's Jr./Hardee's, Taco Bell, KFC

Fast-casual: Chipotle, Panera Bread, Starbucks

Sit-down, casual-dining restaurants: Applebee's, TGI Fridays, Cheddar's, Red Lobster, Olive Garden

Fast-casual is the space in between quick service and sit-down casual. It is a step above quick service in terms of quality and experience, but not the full-blown experience of Applebee's or Red Lobster. This has been the most attractive space for new restaurants in the past several years. Customers have gravitated toward this segment because they believe it provides freshness, quality, and value.

We saw an opportunity for ourselves in fast-casual to go, a space that not many other companies occupy. And no one had done it with world-class convenience.

That's what we aspire to be at this point. We're on a whole new journey, one that has galvanized the organization and created excitement within Wawa. There will be obstacles to overcome. But if we don't dream, we won't stretch our capabilities, and we may end up joining the many failing and failed retailers that stopped challenging themselves and coasted on yesterday's accomplishments.

Indeed, convenience retailing is under siege. Supermarkets are open twenty-four hours. Walmart is open twenty-four hours. Walmart is building

Wawa Dream Maker Award

Michael Porcella is a longtime Wawa store associate who truly embodies our values. Based on feedback from customers, managers, and fellow associates, Michael was chosen to receive our Dream Maker Award, the ultimate distinction in our Big Six Values program. We surprised Michael with the honor in 2008 at our annual year-end holiday business meeting, in front of a crowd that included thirteen hundred Wawa associates, Michael's whole store team, and even his parents.

But what made the occasion extra special was the dream package we put together. Michael is a diehard Philadelphia Flyers fan whose passion for hockey was born when the Flyers won the Stanley Cup on his eleventh birthday in 1974. Michael was in awe as he watched Flyers great and future NHL Hall-of-Famer Bernie Parent lead the team to victory that day. So Michael's dream package began with all of the hockey gear to outfit a true Flyers fan, including a personalized Flyers jersey, a vintage Flyers jersey, a Flyers hat, and both the American and Canadian versions of hockey legend Mario Lemieux's rookie cards—Michael's all-time favorite player.

Next, Michael learned that he was the proud owner of four season tickets to see the Flyers and that, for the March 6 game against the Tampa Bay Lightning, he would watch the pregame warm-up from the Flyers bench and ride the Zamboni machine during intermission.

And then, to top it all off, Flyers great Bernie Parent, the player who sparked Michael's passion for hockey back in 1974, walked onstage and presented Michael with a full set of Wawa values pins and a replica of the Stanley Cup.

It was a moment that confirmed forever that Wawa is truly a place where dreams can come true!

bigger *and* smaller stores. It seems like there are Walgreen's and CVS stores at every busy intersection in America. Many of those locations are open twenty-four hours a day, well stocked with convenience store items. And now we also have dollar stores that are opening everywhere, imitating value-priced convenience stores. Supermarkets and hypermarkets (Costco, BJ's, Sam's Club, etc.) sell gas. Everyone wants a piece of convenience.

In this hypercompetitive environment, we want to protect our market share but at the same time expand our space. That's another part of the reason for our new dream.

Staying unique is another dream. We don't want to be like McDonald's going against Burger King, or Home Depot going against Lowe's. We want to be like Cirque du Soleil competing against . . . no one. No experience on earth is quite like Cirque du Soleil. Our dream is to own a similarly uncontested space. That's the concept of finding your "Blue Ocean."

The most challenging part of reaching these goals is keeping people aligned and motivated along the way, letting them know exactly what their role is on the journey. At Wawa through the years, we've communicated on a regular basis via video (formerly called WATV, the Wawa Associates Television Network), newsletters, intranet, and quarterly reports, so there is no doubt about where we're headed and what we've achieved so far. Before we embark upon a strategy, we test it and get feedback. We want people to feel good about it. Every quarter, Wawa leaders conduct daylong business sessions with our general managers during which we update them as to where the business is and where it needs to go next. We probably spend a lot more time up front selling, communicating, and aligning our people at all levels with our strategy than most companies do.

Having a dream and working as a team to make it a reality gives all of us at Wawa a great reason to be excited when we come to work every day.

SERVE OTHERS

We've always told our associates in the stores, "You may brew coffee, make hoagies, pump gas, work the register, or clean the restrooms, but when you come to work at Wawa, you're doing something far more important, and that's helping your friends and neighbors have a better day. There's no better calling."

Our business is all about serving others; it's a vital part of the Wood family DNA.

Dick Wood's father, Richard D. Wood, was instrumental in helping Children's Hospital in Philadelphia grow and expand. Dick himself has been on the board of many, many nonprofit institutions, including Children's Hospital, helping them grow and expand. This willingness and appetite for giving back to the community gave Wawa life and strength.

Now the passion to serve has permeated every level of our organization. Almost every major charitable cause we're engaged in today was inaugurated by individual associates or groups of associates rather than top executives. Our rank-and-file associates demonstrate a tremendous passion for the Susan G. Komen Race for the Cure, Juvenile Diabetes, the Special Olympics, USO, the Food Bank of Philadelphia, Operation Warm, the American Red Cross, and many other causes.

Wawa associates have been supporting Operation Brotherly Love since 2009. This amazing event is purely grass roots. It started when Adam Schall, Wawa's planning and analysis director, and a group of his close friends began reaching out to shelters, visiting them before the holidays and bringing gifts, candy, and most important, giving their time to show the kids that someone cared about them. As the number of shelters they visited grew, so did their desire to help. They recruited others, and sought to centralize the event and bring the families together.

A Cup of Kindness

The Wawa coffee cart started rolling at Children's Hospital in 1992 when Wawa associates began stocking and staffing a cart providing simple comforts to the parents of patients at Children's Hospital. It was the idea of two Red Roof associates—Barbara Bratton and Mandy Lain—plus a group of our Center City store managers who wanted more direct involvement with Children's Hospital.

Today, the cart operates seven days a week, and serves about 100 cups of complementary Wawa coffee each night, or about 42,000 cups a year along with Wawa iced teas and juices. Each "Wawa Wednesday," store associates continue to staff the cart.

Now Operation Brotherly Love sponsors a full-blown holiday carnival for kids that supports more than five-hundred Philadelphia-area families in need, and treats more than fifteen-hundred children to games, balloon artists, face painters, arts and crafts, dancing, entertainers, and a family photo station. Every child receives a brand new gift and a brand new winter coat courtesy of Operation Warm.

It has become one of the largest holiday events for families in need in the Philadelphia region, and is supported by thousands of volunteers, several corporations, and the mayor's office. Every year, Wawa's support and number of volunteers grows, and now tops five hundred.

Wawa's Mandy Lain is another associate who sparked a program that has grown far beyond her expectations. For many years, Mandy has been sending coffee to US Armed Forces servicemen and women in response to the many letters and emails we receive from our troops. Others at Wawa got involved, and the program grew to the point where we shipped twenty-five hundred individual care packages of coffee, letters, and toiletries to our troops, often throwing in Wawa T-shirts and in one case a banner the troops hung at their base.

Every year on Mother's Day, we show up at 4:00 a.m. to support the Susan G. Komen Foundation's Race for the Cure in Philadelphia. We create a festive atmosphere and serve 50,000 doughnuts, 50,000 juices and teas, and 50,000 bananas.

These efforts are important to many of us on a personal level. For example, thanks to our involvement in Komen's work to alleviate suffering from breast cancer, I became very committed to learning about appropriate treatments and support. When I see the breast cancer survivors coming down the steps in pink at the start of the race, it's awe-inspiring. We see the inscriptions on the backs of the shirts—WALKING IN MEMORY OF . . . or IN SUPPORT OF . . . —and we cry with them.

"When the race first came to Philadelphia, no one in those days dared talk about breast cancer," says Elaine I. Grobman, chief executive officer of Susan G. Komen Philadelphia. "When we went to Wawa and told them about this vision that we had—remember no one even knew what Race for the Cure was then—they believed in us."

The first year attracted 1,983 runners and we showed up with drinks, muffins, and pretzels. We earmarked our first grant to Komen through our corporate charities committee. As the years passed, Komen grew larger in Philadelphia and we contributed to the vision that it could become the largest breast cancer event in the Delaware Valley.

"Wawa is an icon at the Race for the Cure," Elaine says. "When people arrive at Race for the Cure, they want to know, 'Where's the Wawa tent?' They know that the volunteers inside it are Wawa volunteers. They're part of the corporate message of working with the community and giving back and constantly saying, 'What more can I do?'"

The motivation to serve also comes from past tragedies that have touched the Wawa family. One of those affected was Chrissy Callahan.

Chrissy was a general manager at one of our stores in Bethany Beach, Delaware, when she was diagnosed with breast cancer. She continued to work while getting treatment. When she was first treated with chemotherapy all of the associates in the store shaved their heads to show their solidarity. About five months later she went to talk to her friend Maureen Pimble, who was managing another store in Rehoboth Beach, Delaware.

"She was more serious than I had ever seen her," Maureen said. "The cancer had gotten worse and she had to get a double mastectomy. A couple of us went to the hospital and stayed with her for two days while she went through all that."

When the treatments started to get more expensive, the associates and managers in the area started having bake sales, and raised thousands of dollars. When her condition worsened, managers started taking turns taking dinner to Chrissy's family because she no longer had the strength to cook.

On May 30, 2006, Chrissy passed away, leaving a seven-year-old daughter, an eleven-year-old daughter, and a seventeen-year-old son.

Today, Maureen drives to Philadelphia annually with Wawa volunteers to staff the Wawa bakery tent at the Race for the Cure in Chrissy's honor. There are a lot of Wawa survivors in the tent, and this story reflects the way the Wawa family rallies around to help other members of the flock. It's the Wawa way.

Every Wawa associate has their own favorite examples of Wawa's commitment to serving others. Mine include our ten-day-long Wawa Welcome America! festivals held around the Fourth of July in Philadelphia, at which we build hoagies for troops, send out USO care packages, to read to children, and much more; our work with Eden Autism Services in Princeton, New Jersey, which started in 1981 when we hired Ariel Shriner, who we believe was the first American with autism to ever work in the retail sector; and our work to support kids suffering from epilepsy-related disorders who are on the ketogenic diet: We provide free heavy Wawa cream that forces the body to constantly burn fat thereby staving off often crippling seizures.

At Wawa, just as we keep searching for new treats to add to our menu, we keep discovering new ways to serve the people of our communities. We never intend to stop.

Ari, Eden, and Wawa

In 2011, Wawa hosted a celebration honoring thirty years of Ariel Shiner's work. Shiner has been a loyal and valuable Wawa associate for all of his adult life, serving at the Wawa food market in Princeton, New Jersey. Shiner began working at Wawa in 1981 through a pilot program with the Eden Institute for Autism located in Princeton.

Shiner began his career with Wawa stocking shelves, preparing coffee, and pricing candy. Today, decades later, he still faithfully shows up for work at the Princeton Wawa and does an outstanding job. Shiner is considered a pioneer in opening the door for people with autism to gain employment.

Due to Shiner's success at Wawa, Eden Work Education and Resource Centers (WERCs) was founded in 1983. Eden WERCs is the adult employment division of the Eden Family of Services, a not-for-profit organization dedicated to providing lifespan supports for children and adults with autism. Today, Wawa continues to work with Eden and other organizations like it to provide employment opportunities to talented individuals regardless of what some consider their disabilities.

SEIZE OPPORTUNITIES

Many of Wawa's greatest successes didn't come out of the strategic plan. They came from looking at what's happening today, evaluating that against the strategic plan, and then asking ourselves, "Is the strategic plan aligned with the world as we know it today? If not, how do we need to change our plans to reflect the new reality?"

In 2008, as the economy plummeted with the failures of the banking and mortgage industries, rising unemployment, and the loss of faith in Wall Street, our business was seriously impacted. We had a very aggressive plan to open stores in Florida around this time. But Florida was hit pretty hard by the economic slowdown. The window of opportunity had slammed shut. We adjusted the timing on our move to Florida to wait until conditions were better.

In my mind, strength has never come from rigidity—it's been spurred by flexibility. We may have a navigation system that tells us where to head, but when we encounter traffic and detours along the way, we need to be able to reroute.

Sometimes we seize windows of opportunity in less conspicuous ways.

When we first installed ATM machines in our stores, almost every other retailer was charging at least one dollar per ATM transaction. But we saw this as an opportunity to really be a friend and give customers one more reason to come to Wawa. We made ATM transactions surcharge free in Wawa stores.

People thought we were nuts! Our own banking partners thought we were nuts! They failed to understand an important part of the public's attraction to Wawa. It was a good idea to have people get their money for nothing from the ATM machine, because then they were free to spend it . . . in the store.

And it worked. People spent money as soon as they got their hands on it! Fifty percent of every free ATM transaction at Wawa resulted in cash from that machine being spent moments later in the store.

It was, after all, their money. To give them access to their own money for free was the right thing to do, and it made it us different.

We never intended to become a bank or compete with banks, but we ended up creating the highest volume ATM network in Philadelphia, including some of the highest volume ATM machines. Years later, free ATM transactions continue to create a tremendous halo over the Wawa brand—and bring in extra traffic that's worth its weight in gold.

In April 2010, Wawa's ATM transactions surpassed an extraordinary milestone: the one-billionth transaction using Wawa's surcharge-free PNC Bank ATMs. Through the years, Wawa and PNC customers have collectively saved more than $1.3 billion in potential ATM surcharge fees.

About a decade before that, a group of Wawa leaders visited Great Britain, most notably Tesco, which operates hypermarkets, supermarkets, and convenience retail stores with and without gas throughout the United Kingdom. We remember talking to general managers in these incredibly busy stores about their inventory-ordering processes. "How do you get enough product in the stores?" we asked.

"If we count it," a general manager said, "the product comes."

"What do you mean by that?" we asked.

"We count the inventory we have on hand, enter it into the computer, and the computer completes the order."

That made such simple sense, we created a vision for logistics at Wawa that would be as simple as what we saw work so brilliantly in Great Britain.

Here's an example of why logistics are so important for Wawa. Ours is a weather-driven business. Following a particularly hot summer weekend, our stores would be depleted. We would be so low on product that customers would walk in and see big holes on the shelves. At the time, like most retailers, we had a traditional system that relied on someone's large warehouse and their decision to make deliveries once or twice a week based on their convenience, not our need.

We asked our distributor, McLane, to build a distribution facility that supported only Wawa. We would no longer be at the mercy of another chain's needs or a distributor's convenience. No other convenience retailer in the Philadelphia marketplace had the critical mass to make that system work. Now our centralized distribution system delivers nonperishables either twice a week or, in the highest volume locations, every other day to every Wawa store. We also installed a fresh channel system whereby we deliver fresh, perishable products overnight to every store. And we put SAP technology into place so that the system, not the associates, does most of the ordering.

Our forte, our core capability, is opening and operating stores. That's where we want to put our capital. We don't have capabilities in terms of running warehouses, commissaries, or fuel storage tanks. We let others use their capital and we make sure that they get an adequate return—a win-win for them—so they can succeed as well.

These win-win situations can be hard to structure because in some cases there aren't established concepts to structure them. The contract with McLane was huge and it took a long period of negotiating to close. We both learned as we went. It was worth the effort. The partnership we created through those negotiations has been extremely valuable for both parties.

When opportunity knocks, we at Wawa are always listening.

CLIMB MOUNTAINS

Every year, on January 1, we look at the calendar and say, "Here's another year; we're starting over from scratch."

We never know what we'll face in terms of turbulence, adversity, and unforeseen obstacles. There have been years when our people felt we had too many mountains to climb, but as we climbed higher and higher and higher, we always gained strength. As we climbed together, it created teamwork, spirit, and unbreakable bonds.

It's not about being at the top of the mountain; it's the climb up the mountain that's important.

In 1988, in the midst of our Dark Days, we made a counterintuitive proposal embraced by leadership that we should celebrate the top 20 percent of our store general managers by taking them and a guest on a three-night, all-expenses-paid event in their honor. We called this select group of leaders the President's Club.

We took them to the Chateau in Pennsylvania's beautiful Pocono Mountains because the mountains were symbolic of their success. As a special guest speaker, we invited one of the greatest NFL quarterbacks ever, Washington Redskins Super Bowl XVII hero Joe Theismann, to talk to us about being a champion.

As the President's Club grew more ambitious, the leadership team raised a red flag. "We worried this was going to be a very expensive operation," longtime Wawa general counsel and vice president Vince Anderson recalls. And we wondered, what do you really gain by doing all this?

But I had seen this kind of recognition work wonders in the retail apparel business, so we pushed back and overcame the objections.

Since then, the President's Club has become more than just a recognition program or incentive—it has become a valued Wawa tradition. We go to great lengths to celebrate and recognize our top general managers. Each year, we keep searching and striving for new ways to recognize and celebrate our people.

One year, our theme was "Go for the Gold," and the event was held

The Wawa Way

The Quest for the Ring

What Does the President's Club Mean to You?

"For a company to do this for the top 20 percent of its managers and area managers is amazing. The President's Club drives performance, and it makes people really excited about working hard throughout the year. It's the whipped cream and cherry on top of ice cream."

Danielle Brown, 7-Time Inductee

"The President's Club shows how Wawa values people. It proves how much they care. How the company embraces them . . . it encourages them to strive to be better. And the event—it's a dream vacation, all inclusive, recognized as best of the best. You are treated like a king for three and a half days."

Jason Boyer, 2-Time Inductee

"This program shows how the company cares about associates and really makes people feel valued. It makes people feel happier in the workplace; and promotes a sense of belonging."

Carolyn Friel, 1-Time Inductee

"It felt incredible to be inducted and receive my President's Club ring—I felt like Ben Affleck winning the directors award for *Argo*!"

Michael McCarthy, 2-Time Inductee

"The President's Club is a wonderful, unique opportunity to network and celebrate with your colleagues. It allows you to rejoice in the accomplishment of you, your store team, and significant other."

Scott Kent, 14-Time Inductee

"It is such a special moment when your name is called, and you come up on stage and get your ring in front of all your peers and you feel that sense of pride and accomplishment."

Tom Hasiak, 11-Time Inductee

in Jamaica. We had the then president of the Jamaican bobsled team, Tal Stokes, speak to our President's Club inductees about a quality his and the Wawa teams shared: a commitment to being "unreasonable." In their case, they were thought unreasonable for training for a winter sport on a tropical island. In our case, we were thought unreasonable because we sold fresh perishable items, provided quality products, and friendly service 24/7 in an industry known for beer, fuel, and low customer service standards. If you're going to try to do something different, you have to be unreasonable. That's something we encourage at all levels.

Every CEO needs people who understand the pulse of the organization and the very essence of the brand. I learned at The Limited that you need to find individuals to give life and breath to everything you do as an organization. In other words, you need people to create excitement and fun and focus on the soft side of the business. In my case, Lori Bruce and her team in the public relations, culture, and communications department carried out the programs that helped capture the inner core and essence of our brand; that has won the hearts of so many during my quarter of a century tenure at Wawa. Every event and communication, both internally and externally, captured the magic of the business. From Nobody Does It Better, our first recognition program, to the many events that focused on celebrating the Wawa magic, all intended to celebrate associates who made every day special for their customers.

We have a multitude of other recognition programs to encourage our associates to climb their own mountains. These include Goose Bumps, Brand Champions, marketing sales promotions, and service awards. For years we had a Prize Patrol led by our Minister of the Magic, Don Price, in his tuxedo, and Christine McCarthy, our "Sister Sunshine," in a beautiful gown. They were accompanied by musicians and our mascot, Wally Goose, to celebrate individual store associates for achieving excellence in operating standards: a wonderful, wonderful experience shared with our associates and customers alike for many years.

At Wawa, we believe there's always a good reason to celebrate—and always another mountain waiting to be climbed.

REMAIN KIDLIKE

So many businesses mature before their time. Once you become mature, you begin to die, and eventually you leave the landscape. By contrast, businesses that continue to be youthful, experiment, and take risks keep growing and thriving. That's our goal at Wawa: to think like kids, play like kids, and learn from our mistakes as kids do. Once we become risk averse and unwilling to make a mistake or two, the end is in sight.

We constantly have to be a learning organization. Kids never stop learning and we built Wawa to be the same way.

We constantly have to experiment. Some things will work; some won't. Kids will always try new things.

And we like to have fun, which is as kidlike a pursuit as there is. Coloring outside the lines takes us to places that will separate us from other retailers.

I mentioned earlier the huge crayon in my office that I often took along to meetings with me. The crayon symbolized at least two things. First, it reminded me and my colleagues to think big, especially when we were brainstorming solutions to our problems or new ideas to fuel our growth. Second, it evoked the fun, playfulness, and creativity of a child. Kids color outside the lines. And when they fall, they quickly return to the jungle gym or the swing set and get back to having fun again. Adults tend to become cautious, nursing their wounds and withdrawing from life. That's not the Wawa way.

Being kidlike isn't a matter of physical age. We've had people join us

Fun Factory Inventory

The goal of Wawa's Fun Factory is to provide our associates with tools to show one another appreciation and to add fun to every day. Here are a few of the items available to associates of all levels at any time, any of which can be ordered simply through the company intranet:

- **Thank You cards**

- **Happy Birthday cards**

- **Praise cards**—Thank You, Great Job, Awesome

- **Honk It! Peer to Peer Program**—Engages and inspires teams by offering an outlet for recognition

- **Memorable Moments Chart**—Tracks a store's monthly memorable moments

- **Honk! Kazoo**—To add a special Wawa Honk to a memorable moment!

- **"Tell Us About You" Manager Tool**—Enables managers to learn about associates and their recognition preferences

- **Buddy Bingo**—Gives team members time to learn about one another and show appreciation

- **Big Brag Book**—Showcases a store's moments worthy of praise

- **Spin to Learn and Win**—Transforms a whiteboard into a prize wheel or a learning tool

- **Team of the Month Trophy**—Area managers and directors can award the trophy to stores

- **Associate of the Month Kit**—Monthly way to honor outstanding associates

- **Ready, Set, Goal!**—Thermometer shows progress toward store goals

- **Mini Praise Cards**—Small cards to say "Thanks for doing a great job"

after retiring from other careers, having realized there's more to life than sitting on the porch in a rocking chair. They find their niche with us in their seventies or eighties working as coffee hosts or hostesses, serving their friends and neighbors. It makes them younger, and that makes us younger. When we have three or four generations of people working in a store, it is a wonderful experience for everyone.

Of course, there are good reasons why some people, and some companies, become more cautious as they get older. As we became a larger company and felt the demands of presenting a consistent brand, we were naturally driven to protect our product lines. As a result, there's always tension among entrepreneurship, kidlike instincts, and having disciplines and processes. Managing those tensions is one of the key challenges for our leaders.

Southwest Airlines is a great example of a large, thriving business that retains its kidlike impulses, having found ways to combine and balance the need for discipline and the need for spontaneity. Its people are able to have fun on the job because they have great processes that support them. Southwest has always been known for the simplicity of its business model; it flies fewer varieties of planes and keeps every task as elementary as possible.

We're trying to build a similar business at Wawa. That's why we've made fun an integral part of our corporate culture. We even provide dedicated resources for the specific purpose of keeping the fun alive. The Fun Factory and "fun funds" are resources that our general managers can draw upon for pizza parties and in-store celebrations to recognize associate birthdays and milestones. They give the store teams access to resources to recognize "everyday moments," the best things that happen every day in the stores.

In a world where the common tendency is to get a little older—and a little less creative—every day, it takes a special effort to stay kidlike. Celebrating the things that matter most is a vital part of the Wawa way.

THINK BIG BUT ACT SMALL

Karen was an assistant manager in a Wawa store several years ago. We were battling through another staff-crippling flu season, and Karen had worked a double shift, covering for a sick associate and hustling to keep her short-handed store afloat.

Just as Karen was dreaming of going home and falling into a warm bed, the store's door opened one more time. A man carrying a dozen roses walked up to her and said, "These are for you."

Karen was flabbergasted. She assumed the man was confused. He wasn't. The stranger explained:

> You don't remember me, but I came in last night past midnight and I ordered a hoagie. You were really busy, but you stopped and made my sandwich and talked with me for a while. That was a very important meal for me. It was going to be my last meal. I was going to go up to the woods with a hose, turn the exhaust into the car, and have my last meal—and then end it all. But you treated me with such respect, as though you cared about me as a human being. You dropped the things that you were busy doing and you made me feel like I had some worth in this world.
>
> I got to thinking about that. I said to myself, "Maybe I could do the same for somebody else." And so I cut off the engine and pulled the hose out. These roses are here to say "Thank you for giving me my life." Today, I'm starting life anew.

Of course, it's not every day that a Wawa associate literally saves a customer's life. But Wawa is known for having an intimate relationship with its associates and customers, many of whom they see on an everyday basis.

Life happens at Wawa. People fall in love, babies are born, people even get married in the stores. Still others ask to be buried with their Wawa coffee cups.

The little things that happen in our stores matter a great deal to some people. As a company, we have to think about growth to serve our stakeholders, but what feeds that engine is thinking small. What's important is that every single transaction represents friends and neighbors serving friends and neighbors; it's important to be part of a localized community rather than being perceived as a big company.

Success for Wawa is thinking big from a process standpoint, thinking big in terms of how we bring the business together, but at the same time preserving the magic that happens a million times a day in little ways throughout our more than six hundred stores.

The consumer who shops in our store every single day doesn't care, or know, that we're a company with 600+ stores. What they care about and know is their one neighborhood store and the experience they have when they walk in and see friendly, familiar associates. That's what they want from us on a daily basis.

Over the years, when I talked to our customers I heard them repeatedly refer to their favorite store as "my Wawa." They'll drive past one Wawa store to shop at "their Wawa" because of that emotional connection. That store is central to their daily lives.

There is a long list of how these little things made big differences in lives:

- There was the couple in New Jersey who met at two of our gas pumps and later sent us a wedding invitation. We took a picture of "their pumps" and made them a photo blanket with their picture on it. They sent us back a picture of them both snuggling under the blanket.
- There was Autumn McMahon in Maryland, who, while in labor, stopped to get something to eat because she wouldn't be allowed to eat at the hospital. She was a regular customer, and two associates

actually went to the hospital to visit her. Since then, she said they still ask how her son's doing, and they still remember his name, Kieran.

- There was even the woman from Marcus Hook, Pennsylvania, who made one of our associates, Natalie Guerrieri, the beneficiary of her estate when she passed away. Why? She said it was because of the joy Natalie had brought to her every day when she stopped in the store.

Thinking big while still providing the customer with an intimate experience can be quite a business challenge. It's one that only a few companies have really mastered.

It was tough, for instance, to transition into touchscreen ordering. We were thinking big to speed up our customer experience, but it took away a basic human interaction that had become ingrained in people's routines. Initially, both customers and associates didn't like it, but to ease the transition our associates would walk out from behind the deli to help the customers learn the system. Eventually, the regulars got used to it and saw benefits in the speed with which we could move them in and out.

That transition was probably one of the biggest tension points in terms of our "think big, act small" philosophy. In the end, it has worked extremely well for us.

Technology will change over time, stores may grow, products will change. But the connection between our company and our customers doesn't change. There's still nothing we love to hear more than customers using the term "my Wawa."

STAY HUMBLE

The Red Roof is literally an old home made of stone. Inside are rooms with hand-painted, utterly charming drawings, ornate fireplaces, and large oak tables. Unlike a lot of other company headquarters, there are no executive washrooms or executive dining rooms to be found at Wawa. No assigned parking places, either. (Well, at least not until 2013, when we designated the spot closest to the building entrance for an associate in the accounting department, Mary Jo Morris. We'd promised that it would be hers as soon as she reached her eightieth birthday!)

Red Roof is a no-frills environment where everyone is treated in an equal and equitable fashion. Everyone goes by their first name. For Wawa, staying humble starts at the top.

Dick Wood always said it would drive most people nuts trying to understand how our organization works because everyone talks to everyone. Layers of hierarchy and red tape aren't big features of our culture. Junior people don't have to go through official channels to talk to someone in a more senior role. And if you're in a senior role, you won't hesitate to talk directly to people who deliver the Wawa brand experience in the stores, whether they're cashiers or truck drivers.

Wawa lacks the sense of tension or pressure coming from the top of the organization that is found in most companies. Most of the pressure at Wawa is self-imposed. It's team pressure, the kind that comes from not wanting to let down your co-workers. It reflects the fact that everyone feels important knowing what their role is in helping to create our shared success.

Our major company events are fun. Our leaders are the first to be put in humorous, self-deprecating positions, whether that means costumes, comedy skits, or generally embarrassing situations. It's a tradition that Dick Wood always fostered.

In one year-end meeting video, Dick can be seen flying as a Wawa goose across a backdrop of clouds. During a quarterly business update meeting, we staged a Wawa talent contest, for which Dick dressed as Eminem and other executives dressed as Britney Spears, Ozzy Osbourne, Elvis Presley, and "Brand Ranger." For a trade show, we dressed in old-fashioned women's bathing suits, the type with knickers down to the knees.

If you don't think these stunts will help keep you feeling humble, give it a try sometime.

Those stories are funny, but it's our Christmas Day store tour that is our dearest tradition and exemplifies how we try to stay connected to our associates at all levels. Since our stores remain open on Christmas, our executives, managers, and the Wood family spend the day driving from store to store thanking our associates. My wife, Lita, would often get far more attention at these than me, partly because she baked cookies and brownies for the occasion.

"This company can do without me," I always told the associates on Christmas, "but it can never do without our frontline associates who deliver the Wawa brand."

After all, our brand isn't the senior leadership team—it's the 21,000 people who satisfy the needs of half a billion customers a year. That's the brand. They bring the value, and they've got to have confidence in our supervisory and leadership team. We have to break down the barriers. And humility is the best way of doing that.

HAVE FUN

I don't know of any other retailer in the country that does anything like Wawaversaries. These are special days when we celebrate stores that are more than twenty-five years old. People do crazy things, from playing kazoos to offering testimonials to dancing in the aisles. Wawaversaries bring out the best in people as associates and customers share wonderful stories and memories.

We've celebrated as many as fifty Wawaversaries a year. But we don't wait for Wawaversaries to have fun. Working in a Wawa store is hard work. But the associates make it fun by communicating with their friends and neighbors, sharing stories, and telling jokes. You don't always find that at McDonald's or at your local supermarket. But at Wawa, store associates make up a family—and having fun together is something that families do. It's something that happens and it happens naturally.

Wawaversary Checklist

Wawaversaries celebrate a store's anniversary and "key customers" who have been shopping the store since it opened. It's a party Wawa style! Our standard Wawaversary checklist helps stores ensure they have all the elements for a great, meaningful milestone celebration. Here's the list—just in case you've wondered about what goes into making Wawaversaries so very memorable.

- Podium
- History parade (1–14)
- Values icons (6)
- Picture backdrops
- Photo cutouts
- Clappers
- Key customer recognition mugs with one month's worth of coffee
- Goose Bumps awards for long-term associates
- Camera and chips
- Guest of honor sashes (10)
- Wally Goose plush dolls
- Fun Factory supply bag
- Cup cakes
- Cake

Dance Line-up:
- "Cha Cha Slide"
- "We Are Family"
- "Wobble"
- "Follow the Leader"
- "Conga"
- "Cupid Shuffle"
- "Chicken Dance"

In other cases, it's planned. Six years ago, for instance, staff accountant Tom Miller inspired what came to be called Tom Tie Tuesday. He had purchased a number of new ties right before we made our dress code for our headquarters more casual. He decided he would still wear one every Tuesday. As a joke, one year we called Tom down to the company cafeteria, telling him we were going to conduct an ice cream taste test. He found everyone in the cafeteria wearing ties—with Tom's face on each one.

"They are the ugliest things you'd ever want to see," Tom jokes.

We think this brand of humor keeps us all on our toes and makes life around the office just a bit more fun.

NEVER FORGET THE LESSONS FROM THE GEESE

Our logo has always been the Canada goose—*wawa*—and that goes all the way back to when George Wood first summered in Wawa, Pennsylvania.

No marketing consultant would ever recommend the name. In a way, it's a strange choice; it's funny whether you think about its association with either dairy products or retail stores. But it's a wonderful, magical name. Among business entities, it makes us unique.

More important than the sound of our name is the symbolism of the goose. When we think about the essence of our culture, our people, and our leadership style, it embodies the best of the much publicized, "Lessons from the Geese."

There are five major principles in "Lessons from the Geese" that we talk about at Wawa.

1. As each goose flaps its wings, it creates an uplift for the bird following behind it. By flying in a V formation, the whole flock adds 71 percent greater flying range than if one bird flew on its own.

An eagle is certainly a more powerful bird than a goose. It looks more impressive. But it tends to fly on its own rather than in formation with others. The result: Geese fly farther.

At Wawa, we talk a lot about sharing a sense of community that gets us where we're going quicker and easier because we're traveling on the strength of one another.

To get people to fly in formation, we have to set the stage. We have to be patient and persevering. We can't just issue a top-down order and assume that people will buy into it and want to follow. It takes time to educate, communicate, and get people on the same page. The more time we spend up front educating and aligning, the greater the dividends—and the more our people will fly together in formation.

2. When a goose falls out of formation, it feels a drag and resistance flying alone, and will quickly get back in the group to take advantage of the lifting power of the bird ahead of it.

If we have as much sense as geese, we'll stay in formation, and when trouble arises, we'll be willing to accept help from those around us.

Ours is a learning culture. Going all the way back to Camp Wawa and its successor program, Wawa University, we've taught process thinking and servant leadership. That's the best way to help grow people and to help people achieve their goals.

Every leader of Wawa is a teacher. In fact, we've hired a lot of ex-teachers into our business. Leaders need a teacher's point of view. We spend a lot of time teaching and educating because when we do, we carry people along with us.

Education permits people to fly together, in formation, and to take advantage of the lifting power that teamwork creates. Individuals don't have that lifting power—but teams do.

3. When the lead goose gets tired, he rotates back into formation and another goose flies at point position.

The lesson here is that it pays to take turns doing the hard tasks and sharing leadership.

At Wawa, we're not dependent upon any one leader or any small group of leaders. Leaders are at every single level of the organization. Everyone has a responsibility for demonstrating leadership.

Even the best leaders are only human. Leaders have strengths and weaknesses. The longer we're in leadership, the better we recognize our own weaknesses, and we want other people to rise to the occasion. Believe me, the lead goose gets tired—and so do the people around him. I always found it a comfort to know that other geese within the organization could move up front, take responsibility for the point position, and continue the journey.

4. Geese in formation honk from behind to encourage those up front to keep up their speed.

Groups in which encouragement is rampant are able to accomplish much more.

I've often said that one of my biggest jobs at Wawa was to honk. I did that in any number of ways. For example, I always looked for strengths in people, not weaknesses. No one person is good at everything. But if I could find areas where our people had true passion, where they could take us to extraordinary places, that always helped the organization go to distant places.

Of course, when we had to take corrective action, we did. When people veered off the flight plan, we had to bring them back in formation. No one can hire the right people 100 percent of the time. People do occasionally have personal problems that interfere with their work. But the reason geese honk is to encourage their partners. At Wawa, we want to make sure our honking is always encouraging.

5. *When a goose gets sick or wounded, two geese follow it down to the ground and protect it.*

If we have as much sense as geese, we, too, will stand by each other in difficult times as well as when we're strong.

When there is a major community problem, whether it be something all encompassing like a hurricane or as local as a community food bank in need, Wawa shows its essence: friends and neighbors helping friends and neighbors. To be a good corporate citizen, we have to stand by people in the midst of difficult times.

When one of our associates at the store level goes through a difficult circumstance and needs help, we've never abandoned them. Store managers arrange for corporate assistance or fundraisers, depending on the circumstance and need, to get their people through critical situations. Our Associates in Need Fund program is available to help those who request financial help in times of trouble.

These five lessons from geese represent the best of our culture. They've endured through the first five decades of Wawa history and will, I'm sure, take us to different and unknown places in the future. But though the precise destination and the route we're taking may be unknown, I know our journey will be an exciting and fulfilling one, as long as we continue to follow the lessons from geese and the Wawa way they embody.

Meet Wally Goose

They say birds of a feather flock together, and there's no better phrase to describe the partnership between Wawa and Wally Goose. You see, when we at Wawa think back to the beginning of our history, we find that our core beliefs are all fundamentally rooted in our company name.

Wawa is the Lenni Lenape Native American name for a Canada goose. More than a hundred years ago, Wawa's original dairy farm was built on land located in a rural section of Delaware County, Pennsylvania, known as Wawa. Today, Wally Goose is not only the Wawa mascot but a local celebrity, not just in the eyes of our associates, but in the eyes of the Wawa community.

During the 1970s, Wally officially made his first appearances at Wawa, attending all of the company's major events and grand openings. Today, Wally Goose can be seen energizing a crowd, making customers laugh, and exuding the Wawa spirit in fun apparel to match the event—from tuxedos to team jerseys to his red, white, and blue Fourth of July hat!

Wally embodies the importance of working together as a community to achieve our goals. Wally honks to encourage others and stands behind them a hundred percent of the time. That's why we think of Wally as a symbol of all that's best about Wawa.

Wawa flew South July 18, 2012
when it opened its first Florida store,
outside of SeaWorld.

CHAPTER 12

Expanding Wawaland

With Wawa's made-to-order hoagies and hot pretzels, the company born in the Mid-Atlantic states 48 years ago has exploded in Central Florida since opening its first store here 13 months ago. On his many trips to Orlando, Wawa CEO Chris Gheysens would shake his head as he passed the gas stations just outside the airport along Semoran Boulevard. "Every time I rode by there, I'd think to myself, 'Boy, we need to bring some competition to this corner,'" Gheysens said.

—Mark Schlueb, "New Wawa Sparks $2.99 a Gallon Price War near Orlando Airport," *Orlando Sentinel*, August 29, 2013

The latest—and, by some measures, the greatest—turning point in the story of Wawa stores took place not in our native Philadelphia but under the shadows of Mickey Mouse.

For decades, we had built a trusted brand and established Pennsylvania, New Jersey, Maryland, Delaware, and Virginia as Wawaland. Our stores had become nearly unbreakable habits for millions of people.

Historically, we crept out of our home market in the Delaware Valley and into Maryland and Delaware, then farther south to Virginia and north into North Jersey. Florida, by comparison, was a leap strategy.

As we looked at our business almost a decade ago, we felt that to be sustainable over the next twenty to thirty years, we needed a new market. We couldn't go east—we'd be in the Atlantic Ocean! Should we go north? To get real estate for our business, zoned and permitted, particularly to build the modern Wawa offer, fast-casual to go with world-class convenience, is a challenge in highly populated areas. We looked at New York but felt growth there would come too slowly and be too costly. When we looked west of our existing market, we ended up in Sheetz country. We'd have had to leapfrog over Sheetz or compete with Sheetz. That didn't make sense to us. To the south, Sheetz was already in North Carolina, and QuikTrip had leapt from Georgia to South Carolina and we didn't see an opportunity in competing with them, either.

Then we looked at Florida.

In Florida we saw available land, smooth zoning and permitting processes, an economy that had finally bottomed out, a lot of population with a promise of even more migration to come, and a friendly political environment. We found a new market that would provide growth opportunities for decades to come.

That meant it was a monumental moment, not to mention emotional, when we opened our first store in Florida on July 18, 2012, in Orlando, far from our home turf. This represented a dream come true that would have delighted our founder, Grahame Wood.

"What do you suppose your father would have said if he could have seen this day?" I asked Grahame's son Fred Wood, who was at the opening ceremony that day.

"My father was always willing to try new things," Fred told me with a smile. "He wanted to take risks. He wanted to do things differently, and he wanted to have fun."

I loved hearing that answer. I love the idea that what we did when we opened Wawa store 5101 in Orlando was in very much the same entrepreneurial spirit as what Grahame and his associates did on April 16, 1964, when they launched store 1 in Folsom, Pennsylvania.

For Wawa, expanding to Florida was like McDonald's going to China, Walmart going to Japan, or Sweden's IKEA coming to the United States. It was a powerful symbol of the exciting future we're building toward—one in which the traditional values that have made Wawa a beloved fixture in hometowns around the Northeast become a cherished part of daily life in other parts of our country, starting with Florida.

The Wawa store near SeaWorld quickly joined the area's world-famous theme parks as a tourist attraction in its own right. That first week, our store near SeaWorld had lines so long that we decided we needed the kind of velvet ropes you see at a movie theater to contain crowds waiting for the next show.

Charlene Harrell was the general manager of that first Florida store. She recalls:

> The anticipation didn't even compare to what
> happened. Not at all! I got in at four in the morning and
> there were people sitting on the porch waiting. By 6:00 a.m.,
> they were lined up around the building, and by 7:30 they
> were lined up, four across, completely wrapped around the

*building. The parking lot was packed and it felt like the day
after Thanksgiving at a shopping mall!*

Orlando mayor Buddy Dyer, Orange County mayor Teresa Jacobs, and
Florida governor Rick Scott joined Charlene, our president Chris Gheysens,
and me in the official ribbon-cutting ceremony.

"I think Wawa is going to do extremely well here," Governor Scott told
the packed audience. "We are excited this is your sixth state and it will be
your biggest state because our state is going to grow faster than any other
state in the country."

After the formal ceremony, Mayor Dyer and others got a VIP tour of the store.

"I could not move inside the store once it opened. It was pretty tight.
There were a *lot* of people there." Not that he was complaining! "You get to
do a few fun things as mayor," Dyer adds, "and that was a lot of fun."

Frankly, all of us at Wawa were a bit overwhelmed by the sheer
number of folks who showed up that day. Management, associates, and
vendors—whether on-site that day or watching via web video back home in
Philadelphia—everyone was gleefully taken aback.

Every Wawa manager spent time that first couple of days working
in the food service area. John Pineau, who would open another Orlando
Wawa store the following week, announced the ticket numbers for completed
sandwiches using a portable sound system we'd rented for the outdoor event.

John remembers the energy in the building:

> *People were so excited. There was singing and callouts:
> "Hey, who's in the building from New Jersey? Who's in
> the building from Pennsylvania?" People were hooting,
> hollering, smiling, laughing, and connecting with each other
> and with us. It was a great experience for our brand new
> associates.*

On day two, we installed a third sandwich station out of necessity. We brought in more blender units. And there were multiple supply trucks delivering perishable and nonperishable goods.

"We had vendors that didn't leave," Charlene adds. "Tastykake, in particular, because that's a Mid-Atlantic treat, replenished our shelves every hour from a truck on-site because people were buying twenty and thirty pies at a time."

"It was overwhelming," admits store associate Jose Rodriguez, one of our values champions who was on hand to help. "It got to the point where people were actually waiting two hours for a hoagie. It was *that* busy. And the customers did not mind. The associates engaged with the customers, and that's what kept them at bay."

Philadelphia transplants congregated by the soda fountain, and people from New Jersey gathered by the coffee island while they were waiting for their orders. Wawa retirees were there, as were people who had grown up with us in the Mid-Atlantic states and then moved away. It had been part of their morning routine to get coffee and a fresh soft pretzel on the way to school or work, or maybe to drop in for lunch or on the way home for a made-to-order hoagie, soft drink, or a quart of milk. It was a big homecoming for them. Many talked about how they'd waited fifteen years for Wawa to come to Florida.

We met people who'd rented hotel rooms close by so they wouldn't miss opening day. "Wawa is in my blood," said one customer who drove more than two hours for a Wawa Italian Classic® and a Tastykake snack. A Tallahassee-based Wawa fan, whose home was a good five-hour drive from Orlando, made a road trip to have lunch at Wawa. And fan Dave Griffiths organized an event for twenty-five people to taste, in his words, the glory of Wawa: our hoagies, soups, and sides.

"We were humbled by the passion so many others have for us," says Wawa president Chris Gheysens, "and we were thrilled to bring them a taste of home while at the same time meeting so many wonderful new customers for the first time."

During the opening days, Mariann Cunningham, a longtime associate from our Philadelphia stores, was in Orlando to help share the Wawa culture with new associates. "This couple came in," she recalls. "He was an especially big guy—probably seven-foot, two inches. And she was beautiful—brightly colored dress, gorgeous makeup."

The lady stared at Mariann. Then she smiled.

"You're the screensaver on our office computers."

"I've only been here a week," Mariann said. "What are you talking about?"

"Two guys who work with me came in here earlier this week. They got smoothies and took your picture in the store. They passed it around and now you're the wallpaper at our TV station."

We saw some immediate differences among the morning customers in Florida that separated them from those we typically saw back home. In Philadelphia and the Mid-Atlantic states, our morning customers want cigarettes, coffee, and a newspaper. But in Florida they were looking for food: a hot breakfast sandwich, a fresh toasted roll or bakery item. They were not just coming in as convenience store customers; they were coming for breakfast.

Florida customers said, "Wow. This is not your typical convenience store or gas station. This is really different. And it's *clean.*"

The offer was beyond what they expected, and the customer service from our associates was one of the top three reasons why new customers said they kept coming back.

Expanding Wawaland

Opening day in Florida was more than we'd hoped for—exhilarating, festive, delightful. But we didn't rest long on our laurels. We stuck to the plan we'd developed for Florida, opening one new store a week in the region for five straight weeks. The volume wasn't as high with each successive store opening, but it still met or exceeded expectations. Our team was tweaking the stores' design on the fly to meet the demand.

And by the way, Wawa and its customers weren't the only ones to benefit from our amazing opening week in Orlando. Our Lending a Helping Hoagie program, in which we donated proceeds from the first five stores' first week of hoagie sales, produced more than $35,000 for Second Harvest Food Banks in Orlando. And we contributed another $10,000 to community causes in honor of local police and firefighters during our Hoagies for Heroes contest. These programs are typical of the quiet community services we're proud to participate in here at Wawa.

Over the next five years, Wawa will develop a significant business in the Sunshine State with up to a hundred stores in the Central Florida market. As of the end of 2013, we had opened twenty-five stores and employed more than a thousand associates.

If we prove the company's capability and capacity to migrate our brand a thousand miles south and establish a foothold in Florida, that will give us the encouragement to go elsewhere in this country. Today, the store near SeaWorld is an attraction unto itself for tourists from our traditional Mid-Atlantic states. When they get to town, they come to Wawa. And that's the first thing they say when they walk in the door: "We knew Wawa was here, so we wanted to stop in and see the Wawa." They ask our associates to take pictures of and with them.

If anything, we didn't think big enough in Florida. We underestimated our brand and found ourselves in a situation where we immediately and repeatedly needed to expand our capacity and throughput in many of the new stores to keep up with customer demand.

Of course, had we built these stores and customers not come, it would've been a huge drain on profitability and, more important, a huge drain on morale. But we hit the ground running—nimble and agile and willing to make adjustments on the fly.

Florida was an extremely important milestone for our business, a huge test of leadership and a tremendous boost to our organizational confidence. Wherever we go after Florida will be a whole lot less intimidating to the company. We expect it will take the same level of care, if not more, because the results were much more favorable than originally anticipated—and the customer counts in food services were so much higher than what we expected.

We're already looking forward to the next frontier of Wawaland but, if the story of exporting our brand to the Sunshine State is any indication, that move will be deliberative and thoughtful, to ensure it upholds the tradition that has made us successful so far.

. . . . .

The advent of Wawa in Florida produced a host of memorable moments. But those moments were built on a long and difficult process. Moving to Florida took years, thousands of miles in rental cars, hundreds of road meals and motel nights in a really horrendous national economy. All those factors and more played a role in leading us toward the crucial decision.

To examine opportunities for possible geographic expansion, we created a new-markets team that consisted of four people: Bill Strong, representing store operations; Peter Gilligan, the director of real estate; Marty Mager, the real estate finance expert; and real estate manager Brian Pomykacz. Gilligan was in charge.

At that time, popular opinion around Red Roof was that the Carolinas would be our next market. There was, on the other hand, at least one person in management pushing for us to head northwest to Pittsburgh and right into Sheetz's line of fire. He said, "It would be good for us to take on some strong competition."

The rest of us thought otherwise. Why compete with somebody who already competed really well in their market, when there were opportunities in other parts of the country?

The new-markets team studied QuikTrip Corporation. That gave the team access to QuikTrip's expansion wisdom and experience in choosing a new market.

Then they went on the road. As they traveled, they didn't want to register under their real corporate affiliation and tip off competitors, so they became representatives of "Kramerica Industries." *Seinfeld* fans will remember that as the catchall moniker for the ridiculous business pursuits of Jerry's neighbor Cosmo Kramer. They even booked a conference room under that name to hold a meeting at a Homewood Suites. The following December, they received a call from Homewood, which was preparing its annual budget for the upcoming year: "How many events will Kramerica Industries be holding in the coming year?"

Getting market intelligence on our direct competitors—chains such as McDonald's, Starbucks, Chick-fil-A, and Dunkin' Donuts—was incredibly easy. Everywhere the team went, they stopped in stores and talked casually with their people and gained a sense of whether that store was really busy.

"Wow," Bill Strong might say, "this is a really busy McDonald's."

"Oh, yeah! We're the number one McDonald's in town!"

If the location seemed slow, someone on the team said, "You having an off day today?"

And the employees told them, "Nah, it's slow all the time."

Every time that happened, we moved on and saved about $6 million.

Truly, most of the process was really one of elimination. While looking in Kentucky, for instance, we found that a property local planners had zoned as commercial was actually just a farm that received that designation so it could sell diesel fuel to other farms. Not really a Wawa opportunity.

On the other hand, the team learned that a great sign of real estate potential was finding a Home Depot with cows next to it. Home Depot represents people and growth; cows represent available land. Go to Chicago and you'll never find a Home Depot with cows next to it. But in Florida, you'll find plenty of Home Depots with cows nearby.

The goal was to look for metropolitan statistical areas (MSAs) with populations where we could grow not just for a year or two but for decades into the future.

We thought of Columbus to Cincinnati to Indianapolis as a viable triangle, and then maybe adding Cleveland as well. Individually, any one of those cities on the surface seemed as if it might offer opportunity, but none of them was big enough for ten years' worth of growth in and of itself. And when you drove between them, there wasn't a lot except cornfields. Put another way, there were too many cows, not enough Home Depots.

A lot of markets looked good from the outside. Brian's job then became to assess the best real estate opportunities for characteristics such as traffic and population. What corners that were available or could be purchased would be acceptable to Wawa? Was there an old antique store or a shuttered gas station that might be for sale?

Analyzing the development process was also an important step. For example, in Delaware County, near Philadelphia, there are forty-nine different municipalities, each with its own commercial building ordinances. We had to research local regulations everywhere we went to learn whether our use could get approved, if we needed special exceptions, and what the overall timing might look like.

In Philadelphia, a new Wawa store takes about three years to get approved. By comparison, the reports we were getting about Florida said the same process might take just ten to fourteen months.

"We didn't believe that," Brian says. "Nothing could be that fast."

Chicago was like Philadelphia, with a minimum two-year process that was also highly political. Ohio was kind of in-between, with about an eighteen- to thirty-month process, but there weren't any sites we liked. The Carolinas were more like Florida in that it was an easy process, but there were likely to be architectural issues because stores had to be built behind berms.

By 2007, two years into its assignment, the team had narrowed its recommendations for possible expansion areas to a final four: Chicago, the Ohio Valley, the Carolinas, and Florida. But something had changed back at headquarters. The level of enthusiasm for the team's reports wasn't what it had been. Our concern had shifted from expansion to protecting the markets we were already in.

We decided to officially call a time-out in the game. The economy collapsed a few months later.

In hindsight, it was lucky that we didn't break ground before that happened. It was frustrating, but timing is sometimes the essence of a successful strategy. By comparison, Tesco PLC, a London-based retailer, announced plans in 2006 to break into the US supermarket business in California, Arizona, and Nevada, boasting about all its market research. According to the *Los Angeles Times*, five years and billions of dollars in losses later, the company waved the white flag of surrender. And in September 2013, they announced intentions to sell to Yucaipa Companies, a Los Angeles private equity firm.

The Tesco story was a stark reminder of the fact that, when you take your show on the road, there are no guarantees. Especially when you expand away from home. We were smart to keep our powder dry during a time of economic decline.

A year had passed when, in mid-2009, we decided it was time to get back to work, and fast. We were thinking about mistakes we'd made when we moved to Virginia in 1998, when we didn't open enough stores fast enough, built them too far apart, and didn't consider the dynamics of the market. The consequence was that we did not create enough brand recognition.

Marty Mager's job on the team was to look for hidden risks that we needed to consider. We were on the verge of making a billion-dollar investment over a ten-year period. Beyond running the cash flows, Marty studied whether there were any odd cigarette laws in the states we were considering. Were there any odd fueling laws? And what about peculiarities in the state's labor rules? Any of these booby traps could make a particular expansion zone into a major headache.

Working in the open this time, the team met with economic development officials in each potential market and laid out the Wawa story: "We're looking for a market where we can build at least fifty to a hundred new stores. Tell us about your town, what's going on, and where the growth is." We had them bring in their community's best developers to pitch us. We met professionals who were more knowledgeable about their home markets than we were, and we brought them in to talk with us about growth, zoning, and the permit process.

In Chicago, the agents came up with thirty-five sites. Out of those thirty-five, we saw only ten to fifteen as viable for Wawa. The numbers were similar in Columbus.

When we returned to Florida for presentations, real estate firm CB

Richard Ellis recommended 175 sites across the I-4 corridor from Tampa on the west coast, to Orlando, and on to the east coast. Independently, we identified even more sites than they did and walked out with close to two hundred locations we thought we could use.

Florida also offered immense quantities of people. There were 9 million people in Chicago, but put Orlando and Tampa together and that added up to 6 million people in a considerably friendlier, more cooperative business climate in search of partners with whom they could do new things.

The choice became clear. By late 2009, the new-markets team had taken management from Red Roof on Florida tours and showed them real sites. From there, it was the exact opposite of our approach to Virginia: We signed nine deals for land in fall 2010, followed by forty-two in 2011, twenty-eight in 2012, and and twenty-two in 2013. To put that in perspective, the typical real estate manager does between three and five leases a year. The land development process on the first batch of Florida sites we put under contract averaged just ten months to get approval. For a real estate pro, it was heaven.

Of course, it also helped that the economy was in the doldrums. The land cost in Central Florida was below that of the markets we were already serving in the Northeast. We also received much better contract terms than we would have four or five years earlier. We could get the time we needed, and we didn't make any deals for which we put hard money down. That can often be an even bigger benefit than lowered prices.

We can open around twenty-four stores a year, so we look at what is available as far as which stores will have a permit within that twelve-month period. Then we look at our network plan, asking, "Which stores will serve a market that we need to get into now?" and "Which will project the highest volumes?" We don't necessarily plan to open a new site immediately. Instead, we look for sites that will help us build out the network plan over time.

All of our research and planning culminated in the triumphant opening of our first Florida store in July 2012. All our efforts had apparently paid off, because our Florida stores have been incredibly successful and efficient. We're looking forward to much more growth there in the years to come.

. . . . . .

The lessons we learned from the Dark Days are important. But good times, like the ones we've been experiencing in recent years, offer lessons of their own.

In good times, we never want to take success for granted. The moment we do is guaranteed to be the first moment we have problems. We never forget that good times won't last forever—and never stop worrying about the challenges, obstacles, and disappointments we're sure to encounter along the way. That's one reason we invest in people, product, and place in both the good times and the bad times.

Good times offer an opportunity to renew our investment in the business. For example, we remodel older stores that don't look contemporary and don't reflect the current brand. We close old stores in good times and bad if they don't embody the Wawa brand experience. If we've outgrown stores, as painful as it may be, we close them and vacate markets that don't work for us.

In good times, it's also important not to get caught up on growth for the sake of growth. We've had periods in our history when we've been able to increase our sales dramatically. From 1992 to 1998, our sales grew 40 percent, even as we decreased the number of Wawa stores.

This can be a moment of danger. We've all seen retail chains of the moment that go on a growth rampage as sales and profits grow. Management convinces itself that success will continue indefinitely. At Wawa, we probably worry more when business is good than when it's bad, because we know it's not going to continue that way forever. We need to keep our associates on the edge of their seats, regularly renewing and refreshing the business. When life is good and profits are great, it takes the edge off the business and it can take the edge off our people. We try to be even-keeled and humble. We take the good, but we try not to become euphoric.

The same philosophy explains why we don't buy competing businesses. We don't make acquisitions even though we've had the financial ability to do so because we want to stay true to our brand. We've had opportunities to expand in other countries, to franchise the business, to license the business— we simply won't do it. Those moves are not true to our brand.

The good times aren't for spreading our wings and taking needless risks. They're for building a strong foundation and investing in the business as we have with new technology and enhanced distribution facilities.

As we expand Wawaland in the future, we will do so on our own terms, with an attitude of humility, steadiness, tenacity, and thoughtful long-term growth. That attitude is an important element of the Wawa way.

April 16th is "Wawa Day," a day that celebrates our history and our roots as well as our exciting future ahead.

CHAPTER 13

Celebrating a Happy 50th!

"Why are people so fanatical about what appears, to the rest of the country, to be a glorified service station? 'We take a lot of pride in it because it's ours,' Chris, a 27-year-old from Philadelphia and self-described 'Wawa defender' told ABCNews.com."

— **Rheana Murray, ABC News**

Wawa's 50th Anniversary celebration on April 16, 2014, was a wonderful manifestation of fifty years in the retail business. It was a celebration of our values and culture, but particularly our relationship with almost 700 stores in the Mid-Atlantic and Florida.

Plenty of companies celebrate big anniversaries every year, and a growing number of businesses have anniversaries that reach fifty or more years. But few will match the sheer human scale of emotion and excitement attached to it as ours did. It was loving and warm, reflecting what Wawa means to people and how Wawa fills a role in society.

The event wasn't as much about the millions of hoagies made, billions of gallons of gas sold, or hundreds of stores built. It was all about the relationships built and grown between Wawa stores and our people in the communities we've served for five decades.

The 50th was also a wonderful tribute to our associates, past and present, who have delivered the Wawa brand day-in and day-out for half a century.

Everyone had their own Wawa story to tell! Whether we talked to associates, customers, suppliers, politicians, or the media, everyone shared an intensely personal Wawa story that day. The company wanted to celebrate our underlying reasons for success with the associates and the public, yet what thrilled us most was that customers, who had been part of the Wawa experience, wanted to celebrate it every bit as much as we did. They told us what Wawa means to them on a daily basis and how Wawa has become a part of their lives.

The Wawa Way—the first edition of this book—was released on that day, and seeing it being read for the first time was a wonderful feeling.

FIFTY YEARS!

When the big day arrived, the first scheduled event kicked off at 6:00 a.m. at store no. 1 at 1212 MacDade Boulevard, Folsom, Pennsylvania.

The store—and every real and invented parking space for as far as the eye could see—was packed with customers, media, and associates. Our chairman Dick Wood was there, several members of the Wood

On the Way to the Party,
Chris Gets Taste of Servant Leadership

The big day got off to an unforgettable start for Wawa CEO Chris Gheysens.

While driving in the dusk on Interstate 95 at 5:00 A.M. to store no. 1 for the kickoff of a full day of events, he hit a pothole so big that it nearly engulfed his car! One tire blew out and, as he maneuvered to the road's shoulder, he found three other vehicles and their drivers struggling to deal with the same situation.

Chris needed to change his tire, but, without a change of clothes and a long day ahead of him potentially covered in highway grime, he was hesitant to tackle the job himself. Chris called Lori Bruce to explain he might be late as he waited for roadside service. When Lori heard the news, she surveyed the crowd gathered at store no. 1 and scrambled for a plan B. Public Relations associate, and Wood family member, Thayer Schroeder jumped into his car to fetch Chris for the kickoff celebration and reached him moments later stranded on the side of I-95. When they arrived back at the store, Thayer grabbed Dan Clark from facilities and the two headed back to rescue Chris's car off the highway. Thankfully, Dan and Thayer were able to locate the spare and jack and successfully change the tire on Chris's car. With the assistance of a PenDOT driver, they were able to maneuver the cars back into traffic and get back to the party. The two arrived back at the store just as Chris was getting ready to move on to the next event. Dan returned the keys to Chris with a grin and Chris rolled onto the next big event of the day. "When I saw Thayer," Chris recalls, "he was greasy and dirty and acting like nothing ever happened! I was sitting there, awestruck, thinking 'These guys didn't think twice, despite the day's events (they missed the dedication to Grahame Wood because they were changing the tire). That's as good as it gets! Wawa associates are always willing to help each other!' And that was just the *start* to the day!"

family (spanning three generations) were there, and so was I, as well as our current Wawa CEO Chris Gheysens, store general manager Corey Milano, and Area Manager Kathy Fletcher.

Following our traditional "Wawa Parade Through the Ages" emceed by Kathy, Dick recounted the first transaction his cousin Grahame Wood made fifty years earlier in that very spot. Dick, accompanied by Wood family members, unveiled a tribute plaque dedicated to Grahame.

"Happy Birthday store no. 1!" Dick proclaimed. "I have often said that April 16, 1964, is the singularly most important date in our company's 200-plus-year history.

"The opening of this store laid the foundation for the transition of two family businesses, dairy and textiles, into a retail chain that now serves in excess of one and a quarter million customers a day. In 1964, the textile business was in the process of being liquidated, and the dairy business suffered from a downward sales trend as home delivery routes were rapidly declining. Home delivery customers were changing their purchasing habits to buy milk at the local supermarket. Both family businesses were facing major challenges.

"It was my cousin, Grahame Wood, who came up with the idea to open a store to sell milk products and possibly save the dairy business. He researched the concept and persuaded the board to approve the plan . . .

"By the end of 1964, there were a total of three stores, with the additions of Village Green and Brookhaven. All three stores were successful, and the little enterprise was 'in the black' at the end of 1964.

"One thing is for certain," Dick concluded. "If it weren't for Grahame's vision, we would not be standing here today celebrating. And I believe that if Grahame were here, he would be amazed and proud of how the company has grown."

Next, Dick brought me up to the podium for the official public release of *The Wawa Way*, which simultaneously went on sale in all Wawa stores. An enormous blowup of the book cover was revealed. My role that day was talking about the Wawa Way—the book *and* the culture—and explaining why we do things the way that we do and how. Since our doors opened for the first time in 1964, many things have changed over our 50 year mission, but our values and Grahame's legacy have remained consistent.

Chris followed, personally serving coffee to the first customers of the day and toasting the customers who have made us what we are today.

He said, "On the occasion of our 50th, we wanted to raise our cups to our customers and say, 'Thanks a million,' by giving away more than a million cups of coffee today. We thank you for your incredible loyalty and dedication. We realize we owe our success to all of you. We have so many wonderful customers and we'd like to give a shout out to a few who are here with us today:

"Bill and his well-known pet bird 'Tiki'; loyal customer Lucy; community crossing guard Ray; and others who were present, in this store, the day it opened fifty years ago! Thank you to *all* of our customers who are here with us today!

"As Dick said, this day is dedicated to Grahame Wood, but it is also about celebrating all of our associates, customers, and community to whom who we owe all of our success. Our associates are simply the best in the business. They create wonderful connections with our customers and create family-like experiences every day."

The event concluded with the announcement of The Wawa Foundation, which made its public debut that day. Chris called up representatives of a local community organization, Ridley United Soccer Association, and presented the foundation's first $5,000 check to them.

The Wawa Way

The Wawa Foundation was launched to create even more opportunities for us to positively impact our communities and strengthen the way we do that. We are a part of each community and we serve by giving back to them has always been a strong part of our DNA. The Wawa Foundation is a nonprofit established to encompass all of our charitable giving. We have always believed it is important to be a good neighbor and strengthen our communities, but our new foundation will allow us to create a positive impact in more ways than ever before, starting with our commitment to raise $50 million in five years to support our three key focus areas—health, hunger, and everyday heroes.

In the first year of its existence, The Wawa Foundation contributed more than $10.6 million and received thousands of requests for support. We now believe Wawa will easily *exceed* our initial five-year, $50 million pledge.

· · · · ·

At 8:00 a.m., the same group reconnected for the Philadelphia Center City version of the anniversary party. Joining us were store no. 86 General Manager Ryan Weinsheimer and Area Manager Ron Christensen.

The celebration at 17th and Arch was extraordinary. If we thought the crowd in Folsom was thick for 6:00 a.m., Center City at 8:00 a.m. was beyond incredible. The sheer volume of people that showed up flabbergasted us all. The scene was out of control—in a very good way. And it wasn't just the free cups of coffee that drew people in, although there's no denying it didn't hurt!

There were 50th anniversary store decorations—special hoagie paper, coffee clutches, fountain beverage cups, and unique plastic checkout bags—as well as a live band, games, and fun activities—but free coffee gave the associates a real, tangible, individual way of saying, "Thank you for everything you've meant to us and for your support through the years." It was a small gesture, but when you multiply it by 1.6 million cups given away that day and the connections that took place, it was a great touch.

Wawa Chairman Dick Wood, CEO Chris Gheysens, and I were interviewed by local radio station morning shows via mobile phones and in person by television stations that broadcasted live from the scene.

In addition to repeating many of the central themes of the earlier event and unveiling *The Wawa Way*, the centerpiece at this store was Philadelphia Mayor Michael Nutter, who proclaimed April 16, 2014, to be "Wawa Day" in the city. He read a proclamation that talked about celebrating a hometown company, about marking such a significant milestone, and of how he personally had worked with Wawa through the years.

Mayor Nutter said, in part:

"I'm here to celebrate a hometown company marking a significant milestone—fifty years since the first store opened! Fifty years is certainly a great milestone.

"Over the years, I've had the opportunity to collaborate with Wawa in a variety of ways, from working together through their Welcome America sponsorship, to seeing their thousands of volunteers out at community events.

"Philadelphia, the birthplace of democracy, certainly has a wonderful history, as does Wawa. Wawa has roots in Philadelphia that go back more than 100 years, including business offices, milk depots, and at one time, (the company) delivered Wawa Dairy by horse and wagon!

"Wawa has continued to expand throughout the region and in Philadelphia, employing thousands of people and donating to important community causes. Wawa is truly synonymous with what makes the City of Brotherly Love great—it's a company that stands for the importance of unique community connections, friendships, and the food that our city is known for.

"I think we can all agree that this is a pretty big milestone. In fact, it's so big that I have a proclamation here to officially mark the importance of the day."

Ben Franklin, Philly's much beloved and enduring symbol of revolution, led a toast to Wawa: "To be successful as long as you have, you must have a very strong set of values—something I hold dear—so congratulations on your 50th. And now, will everyone join me for a toast? I ask that we all raise our cups, and I'd like to propose a toast to fifty years of fulfilling lives every day and to the next fifty years of innovation, community connections, and the Wawa Way. Cheers!" After that, we had cake—and "Ben" said to the crowd , I think Charlie (Dick's grandson) should plan the 100th anniversary celebration." (Charlie—age twelve—carried in the sign of store no.1 during the parade that kicked off the ceremony.)

The rest of the day went by in a caffeinated blur, as our associates welcomed customers in record numbers, serving them 1.6 million free cups of coffee, engaging in conversations, and sharing an incredible moment of connection.

The advance news coverage was so widespread and ubiquitous that arriving customers said, "Congratulations" and "Happy Anniversary," to anyone in a Wawa shirt or hat, as if the enterprise were a living, breathing person. And maybe it truly is.

. . . . .

That evening, our annual shareholders and stakeholders meeting took place at Philadelphia's National Constitution Center, the same venue from which we anchor our annual Hoagie Day, our signature event and part of our title sponsorship of the city's 4th of July celebration, "Wawa Welcome America." Naturally, we themed the official business meeting around the milestone 50th anniversary.

A full-scale replica façade of store no. 1 was placed in the National Constitution Center (NCC) atrium as the party centerpiece every guest encountered first. It was also where the super-sized cover of *The Wawa Way* could be found and we handed a regular-size, hardcover copy to everyone who attended.

A giant tent was erected on the Center's lawn, where Wawa Chairman Dick Wood began the festivities by talking about Grahame Wood, our founder. We shared a video with highlights from our half-century of service.

Dick showed "The Legend of Grahame Wood" and then segued into the business portion of the meeting. I ended the meeting by talking about the book and my reasons for wanting to document and share the Wawa Way, and how this milestone was the perfect opportunity to create a lasting way of sharing this great culture with associates and customers for generations to come.

Later inside the NCC, there was an incredible dance party starring a Beatles tribute band, The BeaTells, which was fun for guests of all ages. Mayor Nutter was there and we were also joined by former Pennsylvania Governor Ed Rendell. They officially joined us in introducing The Wawa Foundation for the first time.

We distributed five grants of $50,000 each to The Children's Hospital Philadelphia; the American Red Cross; Philabundance, JDRF, and Liberty USO. We made a sixth donation of $50,000 to the Philadelphia Summer Youth Partnership, which is a charity that both Mayor Nutter and former Governor Rendell are passionate about.

Of course, we can't do anything without hoagies involved, so we presented former Governor Rendell with a giant version of the "Rendelli," a throwback to the original hoagie named for him when he was mayor. We created a namesake sandwich for Mayor Nutter that evening—turkey on wheat with veggie toppings—the "Nutter Classic."

Dick ended the official festivities by declaring that when Grahame Wood opened our first store fifty years ago, he never would have imagined achieving such a milestone or the way that we celebrated it in 2014.

Big celebrations need an equally big cake, so we wheeled out a gigantic one (literally, it was *on wheels!*) that featured a replica of store no. 1, of *The Wawa Way*, and Grahame Wood's face. Then we all ate cake and danced the rest of the night away to the retro sounds of The Beatles. (Why The Beatles? Because they also made their United States debut in 1964.)

Store associates at every level wanted to connect with Dick that night and he stayed on much later than anyone imagined he would, autographing copies of *The Wawa Way*, posing for pictures, shaking hands, hugging, and generally sharing a little one-on-one Wawa magic with as many people as he could before his daughter literally pulled him away because he had a plane to catch.

. . . . .

In the days following our 50th anniversary, Wawa associates shared their thoughts and experiences related to the event on CEO Chris Gheysens' official company blog. Here is a sampling of their most memorable posts:

> *"I was immediately overcome with this sense of happiness and joy. I couldn't keep the excitement inside me, and throughout the day, I couldn't quit smiling. There was so much happiness throughout the entire store. Everyone was filled with it."*

"At the end of the shift, I went in the restroom, looked at myself in the mirror and said, 'Patrick, you were a part of this.' And I immediately welled up with tears of joy."

•

"To all my fellow geese, fly with your head held high because there's no stopping the Wawa super train. Choo, choo. Yay."

•

"I knew it would be a fun day, but with every stop the excitement from the store associates and customers became even more contagious. It was more than just a free cup of coffee on the anniversary. It was about our customers and associates sharing stories and joking, truly connecting while having fun together. Our associates are amazing."

•

"What a fun day. I know our customers will be talking about this for years."

•

"Happy 50th Anniversary, Wawa! In the last twenty-two years I have met some of the most amazing people ever (working here)."

•

"The birthday celebration at our store centered around our customers and associates. I took pictures of the customers a few days in advance and made a collage of their smiling faces. They love their Wawa. "

"Yesterday was an awesome way to celebrate our customers and associates! From the second I walked into the store to help, (our GM) made me feel so welcome and so did all the other associates, even though they were so busy with the demands of the day. They remained remarkably positive all day. The reaction and appreciation of the customers was incredible and made me feel happy to be a part of the Wawa family. A great start to our next fifty years of success!"

•

"It is so sweet to know that Wawa is celebrated by our communities for the day the store was 'born.' I am so glad I was able to be a part of it."

•

"What a day!! Being new to Operations, I set out to visit a couple of stores in each area of Region 2 to visit with our store teams and share the experience of the day's events and celebrations. I knew it would be a fun day, but with every stop the excitement from the store associates and customers became more and more contagious. It was more than just a free cup of coffee on our 50th anniversary, it was about our associates and their customers sharing stories and joking and truly connecting while having fun together. Our associates are truly amazing and are what has always and will always make Wawa so great. Lastly, this day overwhelmingly confirmed that our purpose of Fulfilling Lives Every Day is alive and well and what we do!!!"

The Media Embraces Wawa's 50th Anniversary

"Wawa is more than a place you coincidentally stop by, it's a destination."

Washington Post

The sheer number of print and broadcast stories the 50th anniversary generated, as well as the volume of social-media posts and tweets, was extraordinary.

Excitement about the celebration started building even weeks before the official date, April 16, 2014, when Philadelphia newspaper and magazine reporters started writing about the significance of the historic milestone. They all talked about the special relationship between Wawa and the community of its origin, Greater Philadelphia, and many expressed a personal sense of ownership in our company and its enduring success.

There is no denying it: The press celebrated along with us. It was a feel-good story and there was a collective sense of pride taken in the special nature of something that was born and raised here; something unique that withstood the test of time for fifty years and became woven into the fabric of the community.

We've compiled highlights of many media reports in the pages that follow. Overall, more than seventy-one television news stories ran, 143 print and digital articles were spotlighted, and an additional 440 print and digital announcements were posted. This resulted in a grand slam of more than 176 million print and online views and 4.2 million TV viewers of our anniversary events.

In addition to the sensational traditional media response, we experienced tremendous social-media engagement with thousands of likes, comments, and tweets about how much people love their Wawa!

Yet among these powerful numbers, the number we are most proud of is 23,000, which represents each of our associates who help us continue paving the Wawa Way.

Wild about Wawa: Reporter hits 50 Jersey stores in one long day, lives to tell the tale

"We're wild about Wawa today. New Jersey's favorite convenience store celebrates its 50th anniversary today. *Star-Ledger* and NJ.com food writer Pete Genovese is celebrating the anniversary by visiting 50 Wawa stores."

Jennifer Connic
NJ.com

What it was like to work in Wawa in the 1980s

"The video clip of the 50th birthday celebration from the Wawa store at 17th and Arch had the most hits nationwide of all of the business journal electronic sites—which covers the top 40 markets in the country!"

Lyn Kremer
Publisher of the *Philadelphia Business Journal*

Wawa celebrates its 50th anniversary in the most Wawa way ever

"Today, we celebrate Wawa. That glorious oasis of hot coffee and unlimited possibilities turns 50 today."

Abby Phillip
Washington Post

Wawa celebrates 50 years of keeping customers happy

"An unquestioned business success, it also has achieved a somewhat baffling status for a convenience store: beloved. Effusive customers have created social-media pages and YouTube videos in homage to Wawa while regularly banging out gushing missives about its stores and employees."

Chris Hepp
Philadelphia Inquirer

50 Things About Wawa, for Wawa's 50th Anniversary

"Today is Wawa's 50th Birthday! And to honor the hoagie and drink factory that's saved us from all sort of bouts (mostly with hunger), I've written a solemn letter to you, Wawa, because let's be real: You're worth it."

Josh Kruger
Philadelphia Weekly

'The Wawa Way:' Book details Delco icon's secret to success

"The allure of Wawa, Stoeckel said, is the quality of its products and the friendly environment employees work to create at all of its stores. A trip to Wawa has become an important part of many people's lives."

Vince Sullivan
The Delaware County Daily Times

Editorial: Here's to 50 years of the Wawa Way

"It's not just the coffee. Actually, it is the coffee, but it's more than that.

In many areas of the country, they patronize convenience stores. Maybe they stop at their local 7-Eleven. In central Pennsylvania, they swear allegiance to Sheetz.

Not here in the Philly suburbs, and in particular not in Delco.

We don't visit convenience stores; we make Wawa runs.

Such is the power of the store with the funny name, a brand seared into the consciousness of Delaware Valley customers."

Eric Hartline
The Delaware County Daily Times

Drink today to 50 years of Wawa: Editorial

"Can anyone in South Jersey imagine life without a neighborhood Wawa? When people from the Delaware Valley go on vacation or move away, it's impossible for them to explain how much they miss this trusted friend. 'You mean Wawa's like Dunkin' Donuts? Or Subway? Or 7-Eleven?' they'll ask, and you have to respond, 'No, you just don't get it.'"

South Jersey Times Editorial Board

Heron's Nest

"But it's still the people – and their interaction with loyal customers – that remains at the heart of the "Wawa Way." It also helps when you have your own personal Wawa. At the *Daily Times*, we've been lucky to have one of those quaint old stores within walking distance just a block away.

That's why today, as we have been doing for 50 years, most of the region will be making a "Wawa run."

Phil Heron
The Delaware County Daily Times

In just under three years since our first store
opened, we've opened more than 60 stores and
have more than 2,500 associates in Florida,
our sales and customer count continues to grow,
and, more importantly, we have built strong
customer and community relationships.

CHAPTER 14

Roaring Growth in Florida!

"Most people don't pick a place to live based on the brand of convenience store nearby, but for 26-year-old Shannon Opalka, it's a deal breaker. "I was not going to move here unless they solidified plans for a Wawa in this area," said Opalka, who moved from Pennsylvania to Port Orange a year ago.

Daytona Beach News Journal, **Friday, June 12, 2015**

As you've read, we faced three big challenges in entering Florida in 2012:

1. Could we transpose our mid-Atlantic culture?
2. Would we be welcomed as a fast-casual restaurant with fuel?
3. Could we become part of the daily lives of customers in a state 1,000 miles away from our core marketplace?

In the first year following publication of *The Wawa Way*, we answered all three questions in the affirmative.

We were fortunate that hundreds of experienced, mid-Atlantic-based associates volunteered to go to Florida and be pioneers, putting Wawa on the map first in Orlando, then in the Tampa Bay area to the west. Those new stores are every bit as Wawa as any in our original five-state marketplace. And the associates who went there showed tremendous dedication and commitment, becoming great brand ambassadors in not just communicating and promoting our culture but in finding and hiring a new generation of people who share the same values.

We were confident that we could easily establish ourselves as a gas retailer, because we had the gas out front and a massive number of pumps boasting low prices and no waiting in line. People would come to buy gas, but could we get Floridians to come inside for hoagies, coffee, iced teas, and pretzels?

Again, the answer was yes, as it was hard to keep up with the immediate demand for food service. In key categories such as hoagies, Sizzli breakfast sandwiches, and freshly made specialty beverages, sales equaled or exceeded the highest volume Wawa stores back home.

The pace of the rollout was appropriate. We relocated the right people, the best people, associates that understood the Wawa culture and the Wawa values to Florida. We've all seen respected brands expand too quickly and dilute the quality of their business in the process. That, we would never permit. We could move even faster, but if we do, we run the risk of not delivering the customer a quality experience. In three years, we leapt from no associates and no infrastructure in Florida to more than 2,600.

As this second edition goes to press, we have approximately seventy-five stores open in Florida and our sales per store and overall customer count continue to grow unabated year after year. We have met or exceeded our goals when it comes to customer traffic and building customer relationships.

. . . . .

We feel good about Florida; the customers have been receptive, as has every community we've entered. The longer we are in Florida, the more empowered we feel about accelerating our already ambitious growth plans. That's why, in May 2015, we entered Southwest Florida—Ft. Myers and Cape Coral—opening three new stores in a single day, a new company record.

We *did* have a brief moment of doubt about the sustainability of the Orlando market as we began opening more and more stores there and west to the Tampa Bay area.

When we first entered the market, we were euphoric with the numbers on a per store basis in Orlando. But we didn't completely understand our Florida "trade areas." Usually a store's trade area is considered to be within a four-minute drive, which is drawn in a tight circumference around the location. But the stores were drawing a much wider trade area because of all the pent-up demand from loyal Wawa fans. As we opened up more stores, we quickly experienced the per store economics eroding. That became a serious concern: Are we at plan or are we below plan? And what would happen with each of the next few stores to open? Every one of them wasn't going to be a home run. It is critical for our brand to get economies of scale, and just as critical to establish density. As we got about a year into it, there was a reassuring stabilization.

But there were some things we had to fix; specifically, there were two inherent challenges.

First, entering a new market meant creating a new customer base, and we had to figure that out. Philly nostalgia alone does not a business plan make.

And then there was the challenge internally of establishing a beachhead a thousand miles away.

In our first fifty years of business, no Wawa was ever more than a three-hour drive away from our Red Roof headquarters. That was no longer the case, so we now had to make a lot of centralized logistics and marketing decisions. Still, we realized we needed someone on the ground full time, from a marketing perspective, that owned the decisions and processes and developed an innate knowledge of the geography and its unique qualities. We wanted to make a series of great first impressions, which meant continuous special promotions. It meant making sure that we had the products and taste preferences right from the start. It demanded that Operations be at the top of its game. In some cases, we were overinvesting in store labor. And in some cases, we were underinvesting—and slow to react—to some of the new products we introduced and adjustments to the offer we had to make.

CEO Chris Gheysens asked Carol Jensen, our chief marketing officer, to go to Florida and take responsibility for it. And she did. She partnered with Todd Souders, our Florida director of store operations, and the two of them guided the organization through harnessing resources and meeting the need for change head on. Since then, we have put permanent marketing associates on the ground who help us deal with local vendors and ensure service agreements are being met.

Our initial marketing approach, from online to what we promoted in-store, and from the billboards to TV advertising, focused on built-to-order fresh food service. That worked tremendously well, but it overpowered the message that we are also a convenience store. You can come here and get value priced convenience products, too.

As a result, we undersold in those categories and they didn't perform to expectations. They're habit-forming purchases, encouraging repeat visits. We subsequently changed our strategy on beer and cigarettes and altered the assortment of brands and pricing.

The significant change under Carol's leadership—one that paid big dividends—was an overall focus on the beer, fuel, and tobacco categories through enhanced pricing and promotional efforts. This included re-merchandising the beer cave, calling more attention to it, and making it more customer friendly. In addition, from a fuel standpoint, we made certain we had the best value offer around.

And boy did we call attention to this fact with the opening of our store in August 2014 just outside the Orlando International Airport.

FUELING GROWTH IN FLORIDA

On August 29, 2014, we opened our 25th Wawa store in Florida— just outside the Orlando International Airport where there are two fuel stations notoriously known for having the highest gas prices in the country ($5.59 to $5.99 per gallon). Having these as the first and last impression for the area's 57 million annual visitors has been a long time issue for the city's mayor and the community.

We opened with $2.99 fuel pricing next door to these "competitors" with almost as much fanfare and media as our first store opening near SeaWorld. In fact, Wawa's fuel team has referred to the opening as the equivalent of the SeaWorld opening for our fuel brand.

More than 1 million local viewers were presented with fifty-plus news stories related to our opening. Peter King, a national CBS radio correspondent, reported from the scene; we were also front-page news in the *Orlando Sentinel*. Our fuel sales stats were amazing: we exceeded 138,000 gallons in less than three days—a company record! The *Sentinel* wrote, "Wawa has managed to do what neither City Hall, a court battle nor the news media could accomplish."

And while this was not the only Florida opening where we used fuel pricing to generate excitement, it was the highest profile to date—garnering a significant amount of media coverage due to circumstances with local competitors.

Florida reinvented us in terms of our brand becoming more restaurant-oriented with fuel. Ironically, what we've built in Florida, we're now adding in our home mid-Atlantic market. From Philadelphia to Virginia, our newest stores and remodels look very much like the Florida stores. The store design that we're building everywhere today originated in Florida. We learned from that experience and adapted many of the design features.

We listened to our customers. And even though we did plenty of research in terms of what we *thought* customers wanted in Florida, we didn't get real feedback until they shopped our stores. We found that they wanted more and more of the Wawa branded products. We quickly corrected those situations, and we continue to learn in terms of what each marketplace and its customers want.

WELCOME TO *SOUTHWEST* FLORIDA

Opening three stores in Southwest Florida in one day—April 23, 2015—was something we'd never done before or even considered in our fifty previous years. We'd open a store a week, as we did in Orlando, and as many as five over a period of five weeks.

We had opened two stores in a single day before, but always in different markets—never two in the same market, let alone three. Luckily, we opened three stores in Southwest Florida that day, two in Ft. Myers, and one in adjacent Cape Coral. If we'd opened just one, I can't imagine what would have happened. We would have been overrun! That's why we continue to think bigger. It created so much excitement that by day's end, and despite being exhausted, our CEO Chris Gheysens said, "Next we've got to do five!"

The first opening of the day, store no. 5168 at 2370 Colonial Boulevard in Ft. Myers, featured presentations by our Chairman Dick Wood, CEO Chris Gheysens, Florida Governor Rick Scott, Ft. Myers Mayor Randy Henderson, and Chairman of the Lee County Board of County Commissioners Brian Hammond.

"What a day!" Dick said with great joy to an overflowing tent of people, a marching band, firefighters and police officers, politicians, and eager customers, some new, some familiar with us from the mid-Atlantic Wawa stores. "I came to work with this company on June 1, 1970, and if somebody had said to me we were going to be opening three stores in the Ft. Myers, Florida, area on April 23, 2015, I would have said they were ready for the funny farm!"

Governor Scott, who has appeared at a number of Florida Wawa openings starting with the first one in Orlando, spoke next. He was particularly excited to see this store because it's just a short distance from his own home.

"There is so much passion at Wawa," he said. "This will be the closest store to our house, so we'll be here a lot. (My favorite sandwich is) the barbecue pork hoagie. It's a little messy, but it sure tastes good!

"It's exciting what's going on in our state, and Wawa is an example of what's happening. I was excited when Wawa told me they were going to come into Florida. We knew about Wawa from up North, but we never thought they'd grow this fast. For people who like jobs, like I do, every store is another forty-plus jobs. And they're adding 120 jobs today right in our great state!"

Chris Gheysens followed Governor Scott and expanded on not just the number of jobs Wawa created that day but the quality and long-term nature of the associates filling them.

"We've made commitments to associates that we've hired," Chris said, "many of whom started as customer service associates at Wawa and now are running stores or are in management in Orlando and Tampa. These are jobs that will continue to grow as we grow, and these are men and women that will become owners in our company."

When it was Ft. Myers Mayor Randy Henderson's turn, he declared it to officially be "Wawa Day" in his city:

"Whereas April 23, 2015, marks a special day in Wawa's history as Wawa celebrates its launch into the Southwest Florida market with the grand opening of three stores in one day, a first in the company's history, right here in Fort Myers, Governor Scott, myself, Commissioner Hammond, and Councilman Forrest Banks promise you, Mr. Chairman and Mr. CEO, you're going to love this marketplace. You are going to love this marketplace."

. . . . .

At the second opening of the day, store no. 5169 at 12701 S. Cleveland Avenue, Ft. Myers, Wawa customers, frankly, overran the availability of parking at our store and on neighborhood streets. Chris interrupted the ceremonial festivities and used the loudspeaker system to announce, "Folks, if you parked over at the Walgreen's or CVS, as much as we love to have you here, you need to go move your car because it will be towed."

(Even Chris had to park half a mile down the road, on a back access road, and hoof it to the new location.)

. . . . .

Dick Wood was in all his glory at the third and final Southwest Florida opening of the day, store no. 5170 at 1622 NE Pine Island Road, Cape Coral, Florida, as we were met by an entire community of dozens of retired Wawa associates. It made for a unique, reunion party atmosphere that stood out from two already successful grand openings earlier in the day.

The warm welcome from *all* the Southwest Florida locals—residents, politicians, county commissioners, the mayors, and retirees alike—and how happy they were to see us join the community fueled further excitement. The sheer number of people and initial sales felt like SeaWorld 2012 all over again. It had that craziness, volume, long waits, people giving high fives, and Philadelphia pride that we see now wherever we open stores.

CULTURE TRANSFER

One of the elements that was critical in our Florida expansion plan was not just the success of the stores from a dollar-and-cents perspective, but transferring the Wawa culture.

Day one orientation for all new associates is a fun, day-long event, much more than just an onboarding and review of essential company rules. We talk about our values. We do the Chicken Dance (we call it the Goose Dance). We want it to be one of the most fun days in our new associates' careers. As they continue through training, there are more fun events. Our goal is to take thirty strangers and turn them into an interlocking team.

The culmination of training for a new store's grand opening is Family Night, which is a big party with free food, dancing, and games, all in the aisles of the new Wawa store. We say, "Bring your family and get to know your coworkers. Have fun, eat, eat, eat as much as you want, pick up a copy of *The Wawa Way*, party, have a great time."

We want families to understand and support the long hours an associate will put in at Wawa, especially up front.

"It's also a way of creating transparency and comfort that if the associate has a problem," says Florida director of store operations Todd Souder. "They can communicate it and we will work it out together." Let's say that Dad works for us and Mom's employer changes her work hours. Having an open rapport with all of our associates allows us to work together, so they don't have to quit or get frustrated. That's the family atmosphere we strive to cultivate in every Wawa location."

Rachel Aguilar, twenty-seven, is assistant general manager at store no. 5160 in Orlando, but she is also a perfect example of how a job with Wawa can rapidly become a career.

In addition to her job as an AGM, Rachel is what we call an "events champion." She comes out to most Florida grand openings and the Wawa associate Family Nights that precede them. The events champion's assignments include community outreach events, as well as encouraging new store associates and getting them charged up about new store openings. Rachel, who joined us in Orlando as a customer associate in June 2012, takes a particular interest in organizing Wawa running teams for 5K and 10K road races.

"I was just looking for another part-time job," she says. "I saw a store being built two miles from my house, but I had no idea what a Wawa was. In Puerto Rico, where I am from, the word *wawa* is actually the name for a bus. As in, 'I'm going to take the *wawa*.' In the Orlando community where I live, there is a high population of Puerto Ricans. So before 2012, if we saw the word 'Wawa' on a sign we were thinking 'Is this a bus stop? What *is* this?'

"I started doing research, and I thought this was something that I wanted to get involved with right now. Did I realize where it was going to take me and all the opportunities that I would be given? No idea. But I got promoted to shift manager, and then I applied for the first manager in training program in Orlando. I was accepted in the first group in December 2012. By February I was promoted to inventory manager. And within two weeks they said, 'Your strength is really food service,' so I was made a fresh food manager. A year later I was promoted to assistant general manager."

"Now I just want to keep going," she continues. "I'm hoping, in a year or two, I can learn as much as I can and become a general manager in training and get my own store. I want to grow this company to make many more people as excited and passionate about Wawa as I am."

. . . . .

Lakesha Robinson, thirty-six, is a native of Ft. Myers and a customer service associate at store no. 5168.

Before joining Wawa in Ft. Myers, she held customer service positions at 7-Eleven and Handy Food Stores, and was a shift manager at a Goodwill Store.

"I first saw a Wawa in Tampa, when I was a student, and I was like, 'Wawa? What is a Wawa?'" she says. "From the outside I thought it was a gas station. But when I went in, the first thing I noticed was the cleanliness. Immediately, I decided 'I'm going to work for Wawa.' But I was going to school and couldn't work that whole year. When I moved back home to Ft. Myers, I thought 'Man, we need to get a Wawa down here.' Then I saw the 'Coming Soon' sign and I said, 'Oh my god, that's my job!' I applied and then they called me back the same day."

As someone who had worked at more traditional convenience stores, Lakesha recognized during her weeks of Wawa training how different we really are.

"7-Eleven and the others are convenience stores. Wawa is not," she says. "Wawas are like a family store where they don't just serve you food, they serve you community. They come to serve the community. I never saw anyone that does what Wawa does. If you come in our store, you're not just our customer; you're our family. We're going to treat you like *we* want to be treated, like if you came to *our* house."

THE FUTURE IS NOW. AGAIN.

Florida was our gateway to the South, but it is also the gateway to our future. The Sunshine State was the supreme test; we needed to prove to ourselves that we had the capability to take the Wawa brand on the road, and yes, on to other great places within the continental United States.

That said, Florida taught us that we could adapt to change *quickly*. Florida is the *definition* of change at Wawa. By the end of 2013 we had thirty-three Wawa stores open in Florida. In 2014, we opened thirty-six more and remodeled the original thirty-three in some form or fashion—some more than once! Some, three or four times!

The Florida associates took change in stride: "Sure, no problem!" They assumed that was just part of our culture and now it is.

Anything is possible today. We just have to make certain that we can deliver quality when we do it—that the stores are ready, but more importantly, the people are ready. That really guided a lot of our decisions in Florida— were our associates ready to serve their customers?

We had to be willing to take a long-term point of view, going a thousand miles from home and investing the amount of money we have up front. We began this investment *years* before we opened the first store. This is part of our long-term growth engine for shareholder value.

We're now looking for the next new market. We've assembled a team again, because we know at some point we'll have to go beyond Florida. That's another huge strategic question: Where?

Florida was the right new market and the timing was excellent. The responsiveness to our entry was great. Our timing worked out because the economy was improving as we began to build stores, and we found available space and properties that we couldn't find elsewhere in the country. Florida was ready for us, and we were ready for Florida.

As you read this, there are Wawa real estate associates fanning out across the United States looking for a new market. In some of these prospective markets, we know it might take years to get through zoning and permitting. So when we look at the timelines, if we want to get a store open by the year 2020 in a new market, we will have to make a selection sometime in 2016. That's the plan that we're on for now.

Soaring to new heights on all fronts, from new design prototypes to service offerings, Wawa is committed to fulfilling customers' lives every day.

Where We Go from Here

O ne of the most important decisions a board, and a CEO, ever makes is deciding who will be the CEO's successor.

While CEOs come and go, the most important aspect of Wawa's business is its culture; it is our competitive advantage. Upside-down organizations that believe in servant leadership are resilient; they respect and respond to new leaders. And that's always been the case at Wawa. Yet making a decision as to who will be the next steward of the brand and custodian of the organization is just as important in a stable company as in a troubled one.

When I decided several years ago that I would retire in December 2012, we started a deliberate process of looking for the next CEO. In our fifty years in the retail business, we had had only three CEOs—Grahame Wood, the founding CEO; Dick Wood, who ran this company for more than three decades; and me, for eight years.

When I replaced Dick, there was a lot of discussion about having a family member run the company. But the consensus was that Wawa needed to do what's right and put the needs of the business and all stakeholders first, and that meant that our "lead goose" position no longer needed to be a family member. The most important criterion came down to culture. Dick and the Board agreed on the need for an individual who bled the culture, lived our values, and would be respected by the thousands of associates who worked here. They felt you can always buy technical depth, but it's better to have someone with great cultural understanding to really connect with and empower our people.

As 2012 approached, we looked back at the decision we'd made eight years earlier, and we felt the same criteria would be appropriate this time. We also agreed that the next CEO needed to come from within, and there were several prospective internal candidates for the position. We also value stability, so we wanted someone who had a long runway ahead.

We brought in a consultant, Kathleen Cavallo, PsyD, founder of the Corporate Consulting Group in Sea Girt, New Jersey, to help us think through all the issues relative to succession. We subsequently put everyone on the leadership team through a series of programs, tests, and diagnostics to understand their leadership capabilities, potential, and style. We took a holistic look at our top leadership group and did 360-degree reviews on everyone, receiving feedback from the board, from their peer groups, and most important from the people who already worked for them. Over the next two years, we monitored the performance of several people whom we felt were candidates for the position.

Other CEOs I spoke with offered good advice: "Don't lock in too soon on one player, as the batting order may change. Be open-minded and leave your options open until the time comes when you have to make a decision."

Because I privately gave the board several years' notice, we had time to make a well-considered decision. At every board meeting and executive session, we talked about the top candidates and quietly updated their development plans. The biggest challenge was to avoid an open competition. So although people did know I would be sixty-five sooner or later, and that at some point I would step down, there wasn't an overt battle for my chair.

When it came down to making a decision, we had more than one good candidate. Chris Gheysens was the youngest of the group, and had less experience than the other candidates, but he met the criteria of living our values, understanding our culture, and being someone who could serve all stakeholders of this company for a long time to come.

Chris grew up in Vineland, New Jersey (the heart of Wawaland), the youngest of four boys. He was always inspired by his father who, without formal education, developed a successful career with a series of car washes and a painting business. As a teen, Chris worked in the family businesses. "It was fun," he says, "and I learned a lot, probably more than I even realized, about customer service, general business principles, and hard work. My father was tremendously hard working. He's the hero in my life."

After earning his accounting degree at Villanova University, Chris landed a job with Deloitte & Touche, then one of America's Big Six accounting firms. He quickly discovered a natural affinity for retail, working on the Pep Boys, Reading China & Glass, and Wall Music accounts.

It wasn't long before he was assigned to work with Wawa, where he was first exposed to a culture and a business model different from anything he had seen before.

As Chris reflects, "Working at Deloitte on retail accounts ultimately gave me a deeper appreciation for Wawa's unique place in the retail industry. But only by working at Wawa, in finance and on the front lines with customers and associates in every department, did I fully appreciate how lucky I was to work for such a special company."

Once we announced our decision that Chris Gheysens would become only the fourth CEO of Wawa in our fifty-year history, we gave the organization eighteen months' notice. At first we thought, an eighteen-month transition seems awfully long, but Chris and I both concluded that that time was absolutely valuable. It gave us the opportunity to shape organizational plans for the future; it also gave the organization time to embrace Chris as their new leader.

During my last year, Chris absorbed some of my duties and eased into the title of president, eventually adding CEO as Dick and I had before him. We arranged a logical transition plan for reporting and what his role would be. Rather than an abrupt change in leadership, it was a smooth transition from me to Chris. We met constantly to stay on the same page and to exhibit a seamless posture and platform to the organization.

The eighteen months flew by. When the time came for me to step down and for Chris to assume my responsibilities, the handover felt perfectly natural.

Chris and I come from two completely different backgrounds. Chris came up the financial route; I came up the human resources-people-marketing route. But the big thing we share is a passion for the Wawa brand, the people and the culture, the values and moral compass that make this company what it is.

At Wawa, leaders do step aside, but they don't go away quickly. Dick retired over a decade ago, but he remains as Chairman. Having that continuity after his thirty-plus years as CEO was extremely valuable for me as well as comforting for the organization and the people who work here.

In many case studies about succession, the incumbent CEO doesn't always seek out the retiring CEO, and the retiring CEO doesn't remain involved in the business. Clarity of leadership is important. I recognized when I retired as CEO that there could only be one leader and that I needed to take a back seat; I needed to fall back into the flock.

However, I'm here to support the new CEO and, by supporting the new CEO, I'm supporting the brand and the organization. As vice chairman of Wawa, I fulfill a different role than the one Dick did when he retired in that I'm officially a consultant to Chris, serving him in whatever capacities he'd like. I hope I'll be as helpful to him as Dick was to me.

· · · · ·

What does the future hold for Wawa? No one can say for sure, but here are a few observations.

We've never aspired to be the biggest, just the best at what we do. But our bandwidth and financial situation are such that we're going to grow pretty significantly over the next decade.

I spearheaded Wawa's big move south, but it will be Chris Gheysens and his team who will ultimately create a whole new Wawaland in Florida. It took half a century for us to become the dominant food and fuel retailer in our original five-state trading area; we're going to do it much faster in Florida.

Growth is important because it creates opportunities for our stakeholders: the Wood family and our associate owners. It also supports our communities; we give back to the communities, and that grows shareholder value. If we don't grow, we can't grow value. And when we grow value, we can give back to our stakeholders and the communities we serve.

At the same time that Chris will be pushing farther into Florida and rapidly expanding our presence there, this born-and-bred Jersey boy will undoubtedly be seeking more opportunities to spread Wawa's footprint in North Jersey while upgrading our existing Mid-Atlantic stores to fuel stores. That will cost more money than we have ever spent in our history—not a decision to be taken lightly.

I also imagine that the groundwork we all laid with the new-market team that led us to Florida will continue to pay dividends in the years to come, because Wawa will know how to leap more confidently and successfully into the next new market.

We learned quickly how to enter a distant geographic market. Now can we learn to build profitability? I think we can—and we will.

As leaders of Wawa, Grahame, Dick, and I all made our share of mistakes; I'm sure that Chris will have his own stumbles. But Wawa, unlike Wall Street, is forgiving of executives who make mistakes. I'm the best example of this: I got promoted to the highest job in the company despite having experimented unsuccessfully with adding outside brands to the company's stores.

Looking back, I don't regret a single mistake. I regret maybe not facing up to some of my mistakes sooner because sometimes we get caught up in "Oh, it's great; I'm going to prove the point." Knowing when to pull the plug is an acquired skill. But there was always a win in the end when we asked ourselves, "What did we learn? And what can we avoid in the future that will make us better?"

Businesses that don't acknowledge their mistakes tend to mature too quickly and once they begin to mature, they begin to die. I'm confident that Chris Gheysens won't let that happen to Wawa.

Of course, Wawa is a different company in the twenty-first century than it was in the twentieth century. The culture may be the same, but how we control our destiny is dramatically different. It comes down to knowing what to preserve and what to change, and constantly reassessing the reasons for our success.

Throughout my tenure as CEO, I never tried to act like a typical CEO. Instead, I always viewed my role as that of the custodian of this brand for a period of time, helping people navigate a journey that rewarded them and the business.

I read something years ago that was important to me: "It's not what you achieve; it's the journey that makes life meaningful." I can't tell you today the end result of what I've done or accumulated, but I loved the journey and taking people along with me, and achieving things that I could previously only dream about.

What a wonderful opportunity it was, not only to have worked at Wawa for more than a quarter of a century, but to have been its storyteller, to have helped uncover the magic beneath the brand and put a stake in the ground that hopefully will be a guiding beacon for generations of associates to come.

And I do believe the best is yet to come.

Howard Stoeckel

Wawa, Pennsylvania

Building upon our first 50 years, as we enter our next half century, Chris Gheysens presents a review...

Fulfilling Lives Every Day

Reflections by Chris Gheysens, CEO

I've spent much of my first year as CEO listening to our associates, customers, and community members to more fully understand and articulate the unique role Wawa plays in their lives.

Wawa's journey started almost fifty years ago with the stated goal to simplify customers' daily lives. But from what I see and hear in every store and every neighborhood, we are playing an even more meaningful role in their lives. We're not just adding a dose of convenience or speed; we're creating meaningful personal connections that make a real difference in their lives.

I've come to discover that the special relationships we create with customers, communities, and with each other provide a real social, emotional, and psychological lift. Convenience stores can't do that. Even the best restaurants and hotels don't achieve that level of personal connection. We can, and do, every day. We do more than simplify. We help comfort, support, and fulfill lives, every day.

Fulfilling lives, every day—that's our real purpose. And we've been doing it for years.

Here are a few examples:

It begins with the humble gesture of holding doors. This generates an immediate pay-it-forward cycle of happy feelings played out again and again with thousands of people in hundreds of stores.

There are the smiles, the chitchat, and personal connections inside

THE ROLES OF WAWA ASSOCIATES IN FULFILLING LIVES

Care-giver

Cheer-leader

Craving-tamer

Day-brightener

Family-member

Fun-raiser

Life-saver

Waker-upper

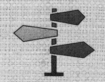

Way-finder

Ear-lender

the store with our associates—a familiarity that creates a lasting feeling of friendship, fulfilling social and emotional needs.

We wear many hats. Think about it. We don't just serve or simplify. Our people are caregivers, cheerleaders, fun raisers, day brighteners, and sometimes even lifesavers. Every day, we fill real psychological needs and deliver on our belief that we all have an obligation to make our communities and this world a better place.

And, of course, there is our 24/7/365 reliability. We are the trusted, daily sanctuary—the unofficial town square and heart of our neighborhoods. We play a role in life's key moments, making good times better and bad times more bearable. From soccer celebrations to power outages and snowstorms, we stand firmly side by side with our friends and neighbors.

I've heard countless stories of family-like connections among our associates and customers—heroic tales of compassion, comfort, community support, and very personal unexpected caring. People don't go to Wawa, they love Wawa. We are a real part of their real lives.

As we head into the next fifty years, it is my hope that the Wawa family will continue to make good on our purpose of fulfilling lives, every day—the Wawa way. We must continue to fulfill physical needs by serving the best cup of coffee in town, and building the freshest hoagies with love, knowing our products will be with people throughout their day. But we must also recognize and strengthen our role in fulfilling their social, emotional, and psychological needs and goals. This is our higher purpose.

All those life moments we create every day with our customers and each other lead to happy, fulfilled, and connected people throughout Wawaland. And we know that happy, connected people make happy, strong, and vibrant communities.

I am humbled to be lead goose and reassured that Howard and 21,000 Wawa associates are behind me "honking" with support.

Afterword

by *Richard D Wood Jr., Chairman*

Howard Stoeckel asked me to write an afterword, what he refers to as "the last word" in his book, *The Wawa Way*. I hold Howard in such high esteem that I was touched and honored to be given this opportunity, which I admittedly approached with a sense of trepidation. However, I agreed to give it a try, so the next few pages will offer my reflections on a life spent in and around this remarkable company.

There is a saying in baseball that coaches usually get too much credit when the team is winning and too much blame when it is losing. Wawa has been winning ever since Grahame Wood opened our first store in Folsom, Pennsylvania, on April 16, 1964. In these pages, Howard has given me far too much credit for the successes I enjoyed as Wawa's CEO, while not fully acknowledging the inspirational role he has played in the company's success. Although he will be annoyed with the recognition, I will take a moment to pay tribute to what he has done for Wawa and its people.

I've worked with hundreds of executives in my career. Not one has come close to Howard when it comes to creativity, vision, and his unique ability to envision an endgame that others don't see until the journey is almost over. This gift of vision is supplemented and enhanced by Howard's awesome communication talents, which are richly on display in this book. It's not about competitive strategies, financial performance, or even the dramatic changes the world of Wawa has undergone since April 16, 1964. It's about the small, human stories—the tales that make Wawa what it is and explain why so many of our associates stay with us for entire careers.

I attended Wawa's annual service awards ceremony in 2013, where we recognized associates whose tenure spanned from fifteen years to forty-five years. More than 225 associates were in attendance, along with an equal number of guests from as far away as Florida and Virginia. The love, the caring, and the emotion that saturated the event were palpable. It was a typical Wawa event, capturing the impact that thousands of intimate stories can have on countless lives—the same impact that *The Wawa Way* celebrates in book form.

I suppose that everyone who reads this book will have a story that stands out. Mine is the account of Grahame Wood, asking to be propped up in the ambulance to see the construction status of the Wawa store being built at the intersection of Twentieth and Tasker Streets.

This occurred shortly after his diagnosis of cancer and just a few weeks before his death in 1982. Grahame approved every store site right up until his death. And no wonder: The stores were his "babies." He was personally invested in every one and in the associates who worked in them.

I vividly recall how Harry McHugh, who was in charge of real estate for Wawa at that time, drove Grahame around during those final months to visit people who had been partners in the growth of the business. It's typical of Grahame that he wanted to leave this world having expressed his gratitude to those who had contributed to Wawa's success. He was a class act throughout, never complaining or asking for sympathy. As one of the hospice workers who cared for Grahame told me, "People die the way they lived." That was certainly true of Grahame.

In 1994, at the thirtieth anniversary celebration of store 1, a video was made in which those closest to Grahame described him. In that video, his son Fred said, "I think my father was driven by witnessing the textile business collapse." I very much agree with Fred's comment. As noted in the chapter "Coining the Convenience Concept," Grahame's entrepreneurial character and motivation were stimulated by the failure of the family's textile business, which in turn led to a flood of new business endeavors, from Wawa kitchens and hydroponic tomatoes to warehouses for produce, deli products, tobacco, and candy, many of them foreshadowing today's supply chain and food service. I think that if Grahame were to come back for ten minutes and see the world of Wawa today he would be pleased.

As Howard recounts in the book, I went on the boards of both the dairy and textile businesses shortly after graduating from law school. At that time, the textile company had no business operations but some serious assets in the form of cash, accounts receivable, major land holdings in southern New Jersey, and a tax loss carried forward from the liquidation of the textile business. The dairy, on the other hand, had a growing business with the stores and was in need of capital to help it grow. I suggested merging the two businesses, and when we did so we succeeded in getting a private-letter ruling from the IRS that the tax loss carried forward could be used to offset the dairy's profits. I think the success of this strategy prompted Grahame to ask me to join Wawa, which I did on June 1, 1970. I've been part of the company ever since, and this extensive tenure has given me a unique perspective on the business.

One of my strongly held beliefs is that transparency drives trust. That's why, in 1982, I started disclosing the compensation of the five highest paid members of management. I believe this kind of openness has created a culture of trust not only with the company's shareholders but also throughout the entire organization.

My mentor was Chester Cadieux, the founder of Tulsa, Oklahoma–based QuikTrip. He was a Wawa board member for more than twenty-five years. (I spent seventeen years on the QuikTrip board in turn.) Chester was instrumental in our decision to close outdated stores and, even more important, in our adoption of the mega-gasoline offer in 1996. To quantitatively appreciate the magnitude of these two strategies, within ten years we were selling more than a billion gallons of gasoline, and while we operate more than 640 stores today, we have opened well over 1,000. Chester is just one example of the fine leadership our board has always provided, adding enormous value to everything they touch at Wawa.

When asked what gives me the most satisfaction about Wawa's success, I always refer to the personal growth of associates who have worked for the company. I include myself in this regard. There are so many amazing examples of individuals who have grown as leaders, managers, and people during their years at Wawa. One example is Karen Owsley, who started her career in 1978 as a clerk in our store reporting department, which existed to track store paperwork. Through the years, Karen drove herself to perfect her technology skills, largely on her own. Her technology prowess has her dealing with highly sophisticated technicians in hotels and resorts where our executives are making complicated presentations. Today, she is a top-notch designer, video editor, and graphics specialist contributing immensely to our ability to track and share the little stories that make Wawa unique, documenting and preserving the company history in a professional, accessible way. There are many stories like Karen's, reflecting the way our close-knit culture and our belief in growing from within help people achieve so much.

If witnessing associates seize the opportunity to grow and develop personally ranks highest on my satisfaction list, a close second is Wawa's role as the glue that holds the founding Wood family together, something that Howard

Growing from Within: Losak Lane

There are many wonderful stories of Wawa associates who have grown as individuals and leaders. In fact, perhaps no one better exemplifies this, or has been more closely linked to the phases of change at Wawa, than Joe Losak. Since 1964, when he started working at store 1 in Folsom, PA as store manager, of store 2 in Aston, and later as Sr. Vice President of Real Estate, Joe has provided leadership that has fueled our growth.

During his 43 years of employment, he held ten different positions, ranging from assistant store manager to senior vice president, ultimately playing a key role in leading the reinvention of the company. Joe helped Wawa become a major player in the petroleum market through selecting and opening gasoline sites, which sold in excess of 1 billion gallons of gasoline in the tenth year after inception. In addition, Joe oversaw the opening of 253 new stores and the remodel of 198 new stores during his tenure as head of Real Estate. His legacy was the transformation of the business from neighborhood sites to larger stores on bigger lots selling fuel and leading the company into the Virginia market.

On the occasion of his retirement in 2007, a landmark was placed outside of store 8027, (formerly Store 2 which was relocated and rebuilt with fuel) in Aston in the form of a street sign naming the street leading into the store—"Losak Lane." This was the first store Joe managed in his career with Wawa and this landmark will forever commemorate the trails he blazed in Wawa history.

describes in detail in this book. All 188 of George Wood's descendants are beneficiaries of a trust that he set up in 1922, which currently owns 41 percent of Wawa. In addition to the trust holdings, another 11 percent is owned outright by about 100 of these descendants. Every November, we all gather at a beneficiaries' meeting, which for the last several years has been held at the Hotel du Pont in Wilmington, Delaware. It is amazing to arrive at this venue and see cousins from the four corners of the continental United States all catching up with each other. Thanks to this wonderful event, I know all my second cousins and my children know their third cousins; and now we have started having fourth cousins in attendance.

One of the beauties of business growth is that it enables us to pay for outstanding talent, which we enjoy in all of our stores and throughout the entire enterprise. At Wawa, we have a quirky compensation system for executives. Base pay is in the bottom quartile of competitive pay ranges, but the remaining parts of the compensation package—annual bonuses plus stock options—are both performance based and team based; and if performance standards are met, compensation moves to the third quartile. When the team wins, everyone on the team wins. Similarly, the ESOP is the major component driving retirement benefits for the entire company. And when the company wins, all stakeholders in the company win—and that's the way we like it at Wawa. In the end, I think the characteristics of private ownership, shared ownership, transparency, and team camaraderie are why the people of Wawa actively look forward to coming to work when they wake up in the morning. They know that each day brings another little story for our customers and associates, assuring that the Wawa way will continue for decades to come—ordinary people doing extraordinary things.

Acknowledgments

I'd like to thank my friend and mentor, Wawa chairman Dick Wood, for his years of support, encouragement, and enthusiasm. And while I never met the company's founder, Grahame Wood, Dick has always kept his cousin's legacy alive and well within the company's culture.

I'd also like to express my deep gratitude to my parents, Howard and Margaret Stoeckel, who stood behind me and have instilled me with a lifetime of confidence and affection.

Where would I be without my dear wife, Lita, who has shared this wonderful Wawa experience with me for more than a quarter century?

To my Wawa family, who gave me an opportunity to serve them for more than twenty-five years, and to be the steward of the brand as their CEO for eight years, thank you for the honor and for all you have done for the company.

Don Price collaborated with me on The Wawa Way. Don retired as a corporate officer in 1999 but remained with us as the Minister of the Magic. As we concluded the writing of this book, Don retired for the second time. There will never be another Minister of the Magic. Don was and is the ultimate storyteller and has always been an inspiration and mentor to me. Don is now Minister of the Magic Emeritus and no one will ever fill his role or occupy his title. Thank you, Don.

I would also like to thank our company historian Maria Thompson and consultant Hugh Braithwaite and Braithwaite Communications. They provided extremely valuable contributions to this project, in addition to their steadfast devotion to the company through the years.

Many, many people gave of their time in interviews to ensure the success of The Wawa Way. I would like to thank all of our associates, community partners and above all our customers in contributing the stories and anecdotes that made the Wawa Way the special story that it is.

I would also like to thank our publishing partners at Running Press, as well as David Wilk at Booktrix and Michael Shatzkin at the Idea Logical Company. Wawa associates Lori Bruce and Thayer Schroeder for shepherding this project from start to finish and Wawa associate Karen Owsley for her work with photos and Christine McCarthy for proofreading.

My co-author, Bob Andelman, patiently helped us through a sometimes daunting process of organization, research, interviews, and writing before ultimately pulling all the parts together. And Karl Weber provided strong independent guidance as the book's editor.

And, of course, I would like to thank all of our Wawa customers and our communities. Without our loyal customers and communities there would be no story to tell.

—Howard Stoeckel

. . . . .

I would also like to thank everyone above, in particular thanking Howard Stoeckel for hiring me, Lori Bruce for finding and recommending me, Thayer Schroeder for being my guide through Wawa culture and fact checking, and my previous co-authors, Vernon Hill (*Fans Not Customers*) at Commerce Bank and Metro Bank, and Bernie Marcus and Arthur Blank (*Built from Scratch*) at the Home Depot for sending me on the path that led to Wawa.

Acknowledgments

I'd also like to thank my longtime agent, Michael Bourret of Dystel & Goderich Literary Management, who wasn't directly involved in *The Wawa Way* but has provided excellent guidance and career advice for more than a decade.

This project would not have happened as smoothly without the magnificent transcription work of Karen Napier, who makes my life so much easier, day after day.

Finally, you can't do intricate work such as this without family support. My eternal gratitude goes out to my wife, Mimi, my daughter, Rachel, and my little terrier buddy, Chase, for being around whenever the workday was done.

—Bob Andelman

The Wawa Way: Milestone Timeline

1964
April 16: Grahame Wood opens the first Wawa food market in Folsom, PA to counter changes in consumer trends that created a decline in dairy home delivery.

1969
53 Stores
Wawa Kitchens: Wawa continually experimented with food service even selling fish and chips, meatloaf and fried chicken.

1972
100 Stores
Wawa opens 100th store, located in Marlton, NJ. Wawa stores are now open 24x7 furthering our commitment to simplifying customers' lives.

1974
131 Stores
The goose and gold background are added to the Wawa logo. A student from Villanova (and part-timer from store 9) wins a contest to design a new logo.

1975
148 Stores
Enterprising Wawa store managers begin brewing and selling fresh coffee, along with sandwiches and hoagies.

1977
170 Stores
Dick Wood becomes President & CEO. Wawa begins sharing ownership with associates through a formal Profit Sharing Plan that later evolves into our Employee Stock Ownership Plan.

1982
259 Stores
Wawa's remodel program separates the deli from the check out increasing speed of service and setting the stage for future growth in food service.

1988
433 Stores
Wawa demonstrates commitment to valuing people through launching first President's Club and "Nobody Does It Better" recognition programs. Wawa University and Camp Wawa are also launched.

1990
482 Stores
This year brings tough economic times. Customer count declines. Several major retail chains file for bankruptcy this year.

1991
490 Stores
Value Pricing begins on major product lines including tobacco, soda and hoagies in an effort to combat tough economic times.

1992
500 Stores
Shorti Hoagie® is launched and Wawa hoagies are "power branded." The first Hoagie Day is held at Philadelphia City Hall on May 7. The hoagie is proclaimed the "Official Sandwich of Philadelphia." The official Wawa Employee Stock Ownership Plan is launched. 500th store opens.

Milestone Timeline

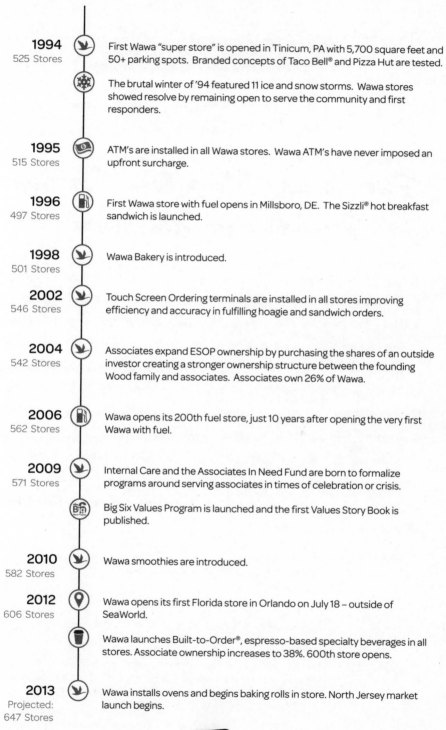

1994
525 Stores

First Wawa "super store" is opened in Tinicum, PA with 5,700 square feet and 50+ parking spots. Branded concepts of Taco Bell® and Pizza Hut are tested.

The brutal winter of '94 featured 11 ice and snow storms. Wawa stores showed resolve by remaining open to serve the community and first responders.

1995
515 Stores

ATM's are installed in all Wawa stores. Wawa ATM's have never imposed an upfront surcharge.

1996
497 Stores

First Wawa store with fuel opens in Millsboro, DE. The Sizzli® hot breakfast sandwich is launched.

1998
501 Stores

Wawa Bakery is introduced.

2002
546 Stores

Touch Screen Ordering terminals are installed in all stores improving efficiency and accuracy in fulfilling hoagie and sandwich orders.

2004
542 Stores

Associates expand ESOP ownership by purchasing the shares of an outside investor creating a stronger ownership structure between the founding Wood family and associates. Associates own 26% of Wawa.

2006
562 Stores

Wawa opens its 200th fuel store, just 10 years after opening the very first Wawa with fuel.

2009
571 Stores

Internal Care and the Associates In Need Fund are born to formalize programs around serving associates in times of celebration or crisis.

Big Six Values Program is launched and the first Values Story Book is published.

2010
582 Stores

Wawa smoothies are introduced.

2012
606 Stores

Wawa opens its first Florida store in Orlando on July 18 – outside of SeaWorld.

Wawa launches Built-to-Order®, espresso-based specialty beverages in all stores. Associate ownership increases to 38%. 600th store opens.

2013
Projected:
647 Stores

Wawa installs ovens and begins baking rolls in store. North Jersey market launch begins.

Friends and Neighbors Serving Friends and Neighbors

The Wawa Way is not simply a motto, a slogan, or the title of a business book—it's a way of life, a guide for valuing people, and a road map for building longstanding community relationships. So it's no coincidence that on the occasion of Wawa's fiftieth anniversary, as this book becomes a reality, that we also formalize our longstanding commitment to our communities by launching the Wawa Foundation. All of the proceeds from sales of this book will be donated to the foundation that will in turn benefit our communities.

So as we celebrate our fiftieth anniversary in retail, we celebrate the stories that brought us to this very exciting chapter, and we also celebrate the newest chapter of our community story—the Wawa Foundation. And more than anything, we celebrate the Wawa way.

Quote Credits